The College Guide to the Internet

Your College Experience, Third Edition, by Gardner/Jewler
Your College Experience, Concise Third Edition, by Gardner/Jewler
Your College Experience, Expanded Workbook Edition, by Gardner/Jewler
Your College Experience, Expanded Reader Edition, by Gardner/Jewler
Learning Success, by Wahlstrom/Williams
The Urban Student, by Thornton/Wahlstrom/Williams
The Commuter Student, by Wahlstrom/Williams
College Study Skills, by Van Blerkom
Orientation to College Learning, by Van Blerkom
Right From the Start, Second Editon, by Holkehoer
The Power to Learn, by Campbell
Foundations: A Reader for College Success, by Gordon/Minnick
Orientation to College, by Steltenpohl/Shipton/Villines
Living and Learning, by Corey/Corey/Corey

Daniel J. Kurland

 Wadsworth Publishing Company

I(T)P® An International Thomson Publishing Company

Belmont, CA • Albany, NY • Bonn • Boston • Cincinnati • Detroit • Johannesburg
London • Madrid • Melbourne • Mexico City • New York • Paris
Singapore • Tokyo • Toronto • Washington

Page Composition: Margarite Reynolds

COPYRIGHT © 1998 by Wadsworth Publishing Company
A Division of International Thomson Publishing Inc.
I(T)P® The ITP logo is a registered trademark under license.

Printed in the United States of America
4 5 6 7 8 9 10

For more information, contact Wadsworth Publishing Company,
10 Davis Drive, Belmont, CA 94002, or electronically at
http://www.thomson.com/wadsworth.html

International Thomson Publishing Europe
Berkshire House 168-173
High Holborn
London, WC1V 7AA, England

International Thomson Editores
Campos Eliseos 385, Piso 7
Col. Polanco
11560 México D.F. México

Thomas Nelson Australia
102 Dodds Street
South Melbourne 3205
Victoria, Australia

International Thomson Publishing Asia
221 Henderson Road
#05-10 Henderson Building
Singapore 0315

Nelson Canada
1120 Birchmount Road
Scarborough, Ontario
Canada M1K 5G4

International Thomson Publishing Japan
Hirakawacho Kyowa Building, 3F
2-2-1 Hirakawacho
Chiyoda-ku, Tokyo 102, Japan

International Thomson Publishing GmbH
Königswinterer Strasse 418
53227 Bonn, Germany

International Thomson Publishing
Southern Africa
Building 18, Constantia Park
240 Old Pretoria Road
Halfway House, 1685 South Africa

ISBN 0-534-54369-3

Contents

iii

Preface

This guide is designed to meet the needs of college students first encountering the Internet.

Section One is based on *The 'Net, the Web, and You: All You Really Need to Know About the Internet ... and a Little Bit More,* by Daniel Kurland. This section is divided into five chapters. Chapter One, "Introduction," suggests the range of Internet resources. Chapter Two, "The Basics," introduces key concepts essential to a discussion of the Internet. Chapter Three, "The Internet as Medium of Communication and Collaboration," discusses individual E-mail and various programs for broader communication dependent upon E-mail. Chapter Four, "The Internet Services," offers short descriptions of each Internet program and indicates how each is used. Chapter Five, "Research and the Internet," examines tactics and techniques for research, in general and on the Internet in particular.

Section Two introduces students to the benefit of using the Internet. The section includes descriptions and contact information for dozens of indexes, newsgroups, mailing lists, and other on-line resources relevant to college success.

Ultimately the best way to discover the Internet is on the Internet. This book is designed to get you started, and to be your companion as you explore.

This is a work, then, both to be read at your leisure for a general understanding, and to be kept by your computer as a reference guide and handbook.

SECTION ONE

Introduction

1

THE INTERNET

The Internet has been portrayed with a variety of images. Allusions are made to road systems ("the electronic superhighway"), Star Trek adventurers ("internauts in cyberspace"), and to a world community (the "electronic global village").

Initially, the Internet might best be seen within the historical development of human communication. At heart, the Internet is merely a new stage in humanity's ongoing attempt to meet people, exchange information, and explore the world of ideas. But it is also more than this.

The Internet is at once a mailbox, a research tool, a vehicle of commerce, and a medium of entertainment. You can send a letter to a colleague in Japan, check the score of the last Bullets game and the progress of a Senate bill, order a present for Aunt Harriet's birthday, listen to a sample track from a new CD, and find a recipe using avocados for supper tonight.

THE INTERNET AND THE COLLEGE STUDENT

Public discussion focuses on the Internet as a burgeoning electronic mall for cyber–consumerism and multimedia entertainment. For students and professors, the Internet has other purposes.

The Internet offers a broad array of academic and academic-related resources:

- professional and governmental archives and databases
- on-line journals
- access to commercial databases and abstract services
- professional discussion via newsgroups, mailing lists, and discussion groups
- academic and public library catalogs
- grant listings and deadlines
- directories of researchers and research projects funded by the federal government
- conference announcements and calls for papers
- academic, government and industry job announcements
- faculty biographies and university course descriptions
- educational and other software

In a broader vein, you can find the latest ferry schedule for Martha's Vineyard, browse advertisements for rafting trips, and download guides to doing your taxes.

Professors have used E-mail to post answer keys and grades, Gopher servers to archive lecture notes, and the World Wide Web to offer problem sets, interactive demonstrations, and supplementary course materials.

For graduate students and researchers, then, the Internet is an important resource for communicating with the community of scholars, for accessing sophisticated databases, for sharing information, and for investigating potential teaching/research programs.

For the undergraduate, the initial use of the Internet may be as a tool for communicating with the professor and other students. A secondary use may be to access information and discussion of real-world applications and policy issues. If you want to learn a particular discipline, study the textbook. If you want to review government documents, or discussion on issues within that discipline, surf the Internet.

The Basics

2

How to Get On

To obtain telephone service, you must subscribe to a telephone company. To access the Internet, you must connect to an Internet provider–a host or gateway providing an on-ramp to the Internet. When a host computer offers a specific service, it is referred to as a server in a client–server relationship.

Most colleges and universities provide some form of Internet access. At one extreme, access may be limited to specific computers in a computing center or laboratory. At the other extreme, wireless access may be available campuswide.

In general, Internet access will entail one of three options:

- direct linkage to the university network
- telephone access via modem to the university network
- telephone access via modem to a local or national commercial provider

If all else fails, Internet services are available from commercial on-line services such as American Online, Compuserve, and Prodigy.

Contact your computing center to assess your options.

INTERNET ADDRESSES

Each account on the Internet is assigned a unique address. House addresses divide the world into physical regions: houses on streets, in towns, in cities. Internet addresses indicate computers on networks within networks. Each level of the network is referred to as a domain. Thus the computer running the FTP program at the National Center for Supercomputing Applications (NCSA) at the University of Illinois at Urbana–Champaign (UIUC) has the address *ftp.ncsa.uiuc.edu*. This is the Internet way of indicating a particular computer *(ftp)* at a particular center (ncsa) within a larger university network *(uiuc)*. The final abbreviation indicates the nature of the account, here an educational institution *(edu)*.

The most common final domain extensions include

edu   educational institutions

gov   government institutions

com   businesses or Internet service providers

mil   military sites

net   administrative organizations of the Internet

org   private organizations

Foreign addresses include an additional two–letter country abbreviation at the end, e.g., *ftp.nsysu.edu.tw*, the address of the FTP program at the National Sun Yat Sen University in Taiwan.

All domain addresses have a numerical Internet Protocol (IP) address equivalent. IP addresses consist of four numbers separated by dots. The notation *141.142.20.50* is the same address as *ftp.ncsa.uiuc.edu*.

MAILING ADDRESSES

Domain addresses are equivalent to street addresses. But street addresses alone are not sufficient to designate the location of a specific individual. Many individuals may live in the same house with the same street address. Similarly, a number of users may access the Internet from the same host, and hence from the same Internet address.

For this reason, the address of an individual user consists of a username and a domain address: *user@domain*, pronounced "user at domain." The username and domain address together make up a complete Internet E–mail address.

UNIFORM RESOURCE LOCATORS (URLs)

Other than for E-mail transactions, most Internet activity involves accessing files on remote computers. Each file or directory on the Internet (that is, on a host computer connected to the Internet) can be designated by a Uniform Resource Locator (URL). URLs indicate

- the program for accessing a file,
- the address of the computer on which a file is located,
- the path to that file within the file directory of that computer, and,
- the name of the file or directory in question.

Thus URLs have the form *protocol://IP Address/file path/filename*. Consider an example:

http://www.utexas.edu/student/lsc/handouts.html

The first part of the address–*http://*–specifies the means of access, here Hypertext Transfer Protocol, associated with the World Wide Web. The address immediate following the double slash–*www.utexas.edu/*–indicates the address of the computer (server) to be accessed.

Terms following single slashes–*student/lsc/*–indicate progressively lower subdirectories on the server. And finally a specific file name–*handouts.html*–is recognizable by the period within the name and the *.html* ending indicating HyperText Markup Language–and is, again, associated with the World Wide Web. (URLs are indicated with *italics* throughout this text.)

There are URLs for all Internet protocols (telnet, FTP, Gopher, WAIS, http) as well as for E-mail addresses, file locations, and newsgroups.

For more information on URLs, see "A Guide to URLs," *http://www.netspace.org/users/dwb/url-guide.html.*

INTERNET SERVICES

As noted earlier, other than for sending and receiving mail, time spent on the Internet generally involves accessing files on other computers. Any data manipulation or real creativity is done off-line on your own machine. There is, however, a wealth of material to be accessed.

All of the materials traditionally stored in a library–photographs and phonograph records, manuscripts and government documents, newspapers and academic journals, financial reports, employment listings, oral history tapes, and recipe collections–can be stored in electronic form. "We live in a world ...," Raymond Kurzweil noted in his keynote address at the Second U.S./Canada Conference on Technology for the Blind, "in which all of our knowledge, all of our creations, all of our insights, all of our ideas, our cultural expressions–pictures, movies, art, sound, music, books, and the secret of life itself–are all being digitized, captured, and understood in sequences of ones and zeroes." And anything stored can be accessed.

The Internet offers a number of approaches to accessing stored materials:

- File transfer protocol (FTP)
- Browsing Gopher menus or World Wide Web pages
- Retrieving documents from WAIS databases

And each of these services has its own search program.

In addition, the Internet incorporates a number of services involving communication, including:

- Electronic mail (E-mail)
- Mailing lists (discussion groups and newsletter subscriptions)
- Newsgroups
- Talk and chat groups

Each of these services is examined in detail in Chapter Three. For additional materials, see the the Internet Learner's Page, *http://www.clark.net/pub/lschank/web/learn.html.*

THE WORLD WIDE WEB: THE SERVICE OF CHOICE

In the past year, the World Wide Web has become the service of choice–if for no other reason than that it combines complex text with vivid graphics, audio, and movies. More importantly, almost all of the other services can be accessed via the Web, or at least by utilizing a Web browser. With this in mind, relevant Web sites are indicated throughout this text.

For those without Web access, all of the services discussed–including World Wide Web pages themselves–can be accessed via

E–mail. (See the reference to *Accessing the Internet by E-mail* in the section on electronic mail, page 11).

FILE FORMATS

Files on the Internet are often encoded, archived, and/or compressed.

Encoded Files

One of the most common means of file transfer is via E-mail. But E-mail files must be in plain ASCII format; neither the binary files generated by word processors nor graphic images can be sent via standard E-mail. (This is not an issue with MIME enabled E–mail or file transfer protocol.) How then can these files be transmitted?

Binary text files can be reformatted as plain ASCII text, but the display attributes (fonts, boldface, and so on) would be lost. The solution to the transmission problem involves encoding the files utilizing ASCII characters. The information necessary for the fonts and display attributes is recaptured by decoding the file back into binary format.

Files can be encoded and decoded using various protocols. Each such protocol is indicated by a file extension. Uuencode, a common format on the Internet, results in *.uue* files.

Archived Files

A number of files can be joined, packed, or archived into a single file for ease of file manipulation. The most common programs for combining files are the UNIX program tar (*.tar*), MS-DOS/Windows PKZIP/PKUNZIP, and Macintosh ZipIt (*.ZIP*) programs. Archived files must be unpacked before use. Archiving enables a number of files, or all files in a directory, to be manipulated with a single command.

Compressed Files

Files can also be compressed to shorten transmission time or to simply save storage space. Compression ratio varies with the type of file. Program files generally compress to about half their size (2:1), data files more than 5:1. The UNIX compress/uncompress program (*.Z*) is often used in conjunction with the archiver tar, resulting in files of the form *.tar.Z. Some programs, such as PKZIP and ZipIt, combine archiving and compression capability. For instructions, refer to "How to Decode and View Binary Messages" on the Usenet newsgroups *alt.binaries.pictures.d* and *new.newusers.questions* and the Frequently Asked Questions file for the newsgroup *comp.compression (http://www.cis.ohio-state.edu/ hypertext/faq/usenet/compression-faq/top.html)*.

GETTING HELP

Computer education has always been a social affair. When in need of help, users ask friends or colleagues who are, generally, only one step ahead in their computer expertise.

For most students, help is as close as their computing center. Many computing centers provide handouts and offer minicourses. Guides to the use of services and software are often posted on university networks.

On-line Guides

An extensive menu of guides to all aspects of the Internet and its resources is maintained by John December (*http://www.december.com/net/tools/index.html*).

Frequently Asked Questions (FAQs)

Responses to frequently asked questions are available as FAQ files. There are FAQs for almost all aspects of Internet content and use:

alt.fan.monty-python FAQ

Anonymous FTP Frequently Asked Questions (FAQ) List

Economists' Resources on the Internet

FAQ: How to find people's E-mail addresses

How to Read Chinese Text on Usenet: FAQ for alt.chinese.text

Copies of FAQs are generally available from the relevant Usenet newsgroup, or are posted on the newsgroups *news.announce.newusers, news.answers,* or *news.newusers.questions.*

FAQs are also archived in various locations. Copies of all FAQs can be browsed at *http://www.cis.ohio-state.edu/hypertext/faq/ usenet/FAQ-List.html* or *http://www.intac.com/FAQ.html*. For instructions on obtaining FAQs by E-mail, and a complete list of Usenet FAQs, send an E-mail letter to

mail-server@rtfm.mit.edu

Leave the subject blank and include the message

send usenet/news.answers/Index

followed by the line

help

with no period or subject heading. FAQs are always a useful starting point for investigating any Internet topic.

RFCs and FYIs

The Internet Engineering Task Force (IETF) provides a series of documents called Requests for Comments (RFCs) on a broad range of Internet topics. While many are highly technical, others offer introductions to major topics. FYIs (For Your Information), a subset of the RFCs, are particularly useful for new users (newbies). FYIs include FAQs and "How To" guides for the various services. FYI: 23, Guide to Network Resource Tools (*http://www.cis.ohio-state.edu/ htbin/rfc/rfc1580.html*) describes all of the Internet services.

An RFC search page is available on the World Wide Web at *http://ds.internic.net/ds/dspg1intdoc.html.*

The Internet as Medium of Communication and Collaboration

3

ELECTRONIC MAIL (E-MAIL): THE INTERNET AS POST OFFICE

Academic research relies on the efforts of a community of scholars. Central to this effort is communication. The major use of the Internet–by scientists as well as by others–is electronic mail and a number of other communications services based on electronic mail.

E–Mail

In many ways, E-mail is truly revolutionary. E-mail travels anywhere in the world in minutes, not days. You can send a document thousands of miles for the price of the phone call to your Internet provider. When you are having trouble getting through to someone on the phone: E-mail. Can't get past a secretary? E-mail.

In other respects, little has changed. You still have to have something to say to someone, and you still have to know that person's address. There is still the excitement of discovering that you have mail–and still the nuisance of wading through junk mail.

The Internet delivery system can overcome many problems, but it is not foolproof. Lines may be down or computer systems may be out. Excessive traffic may slow access to a particular location–and even the Internet cannot surmount an incorrect address. E-mail reports back unknown addresses and problems with delivery, but regular mail is more forgiving of simple errors in addresses. All of the services of the Internet can be accessed via E-mail–albeit often in a very limited manner. For complete instructions, see "Accessing the Internet by E-mail, Doctor Bob's Guide to Offline Internet Access." The document can be obtained by sending an E-mail letter to *mail-server@rtfm.mit.edu* with the message

send usenet/news.answers/internet-services/ access-via-email

with no final punctuation.

Using E-Mail

E-mail programs are part word processor, part mailbox, and part file organizer. With almost all you may

- list mail received and mail sent
- read or delete an item from the list of documents received
- print or save a document as a file
- store frequently used names and addresses
- automatically attach signatures at the end of letters
- send replies, with portions of the original message in the reply
- forward mail by simply readdressing it
- attach other files to mail
- send a document to any number of people at once

The final feature facilitates the postal equivalent of the traditional telephone tree and enables a number of additional services considered below.

While the standard text-interface programs (mail, pine, and elm) are not particularly user-friendly, here, as elsewhere, the command **?** or **help** will usually evoke a list of commands, regardless of the program you are using. A graphic-interface program such as Eudora (Figure 1) greatly simplifies the process.

Social Considerations

Ever resourceful, E-mail users both speed their task and qualify their remarks with acronyms such as BTW (by the way), IMHO (in my

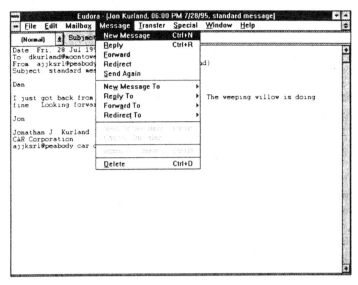

FIGURE 1   Message options on the Eudora mail program for Windows.

humble/honest opinion), FWIW (for what it's worth), and OTOH (on the other hand). Words are stressed by enclosing them in *asterisks*.

Ever playful, E-mail users have also developed a series of symbols (emoticons) to replace voice inflection and facial expressions in their letters. The most well known of these symbols is the smiley, a keyboard-written image indicating delight with an idea: :-)

Finally, users of the Internet constitute their own subculture, one that has definite standards of fair play and respect for others (netiquette). One should not YELL BY WRITING EVERYTHING IN CAPITAL LETTERS nor forward mail to large groups of people (spamming).

Sending E-mail in the privacy of your room, you might think your remarks are truly private. This is hardly the case. E-mail can be read by system administrators or your Internet provider. Mail you send to one person may be forwarded intact–or edited–to others without your knowledge or permission.

Since E-mail messages tend to be shorter than most other correspondence, you must take care not to be vague, ambiguous, or suggestive. Use sarcasm and humor cautiously to avoid misunderstandings.

Finding Addresses

Since there is no definitive Internet, there is no definitive directory of Internet names and addresses. The best way to learn a person's E-mail address is still to call the person on the telephone, or ask someone else. If that fails, you can try a number of search programs examining portions of the system. Try Four11(*http://www.four11.com*) or Yahoo's list of sites (*http://www.yahoo.com/reference/white_pages/ individuals/*).

THE INTERNET AS BULLETIN BOARD, BULL SESSION, AND PARTY LINE

Mailing Lists

The same process by which a single E-mail message can be directed to another person can be used to distribute documents–almost as with traditional mailing lists.

Individuals subscribe by E-mail and receive material periodically via E-mail. (Nonsubscribers can usually request individual items from the mailing list via E-mail.) Since all such mailing list activities involve E-mail, the only software required is an E-mail program.

In many instances, subscription mailing lists are administered by a computer. The first such program was LISTSERV, giving rise to the name *listservers*. Similar programs go by the names *majordomo*, *MAILSERV*, and *listproc.*

Server computers automatically read and respond to requests to start, stop, or pause subscriptions. Most such programs oversee more than one list at a single site. A sure sign that a mailing list is administered by machine is that the contact address refers to one of the above programs. Listservers commonly archive correspondence in log files that can be retrieved by E–mail.

Administrative tasks are usually accomplished by single-word commands–commands that vary with the listserver program involved. An E-mail letter to a listserver with the single word **help** in the body of the letter will usually evoke a reply with a list of appropriate commands.

Mailing lists are used by professional groups, on-line newsletters and magazines, and other information and advocacy services.

Discussion Groups

With mailing lists, a single person or central authority produces documents for distribution to subscribers on a fairly regular basis. Discussion groups are more like a giant bull session. Anyone can contribute a message, which is then forwarded to all subscribers.

Any group of people with a common interest can form a discussion group. Groups have been formed to discuss new software programs, research interests, or simply hobbies or political issues. Many listserver discussion groups are associated with academic organizations, associations, and societies. Some discussion groups forward all correspondence; some are moderated by an individual to assure the relevancy of the discussion; some incorporate messages into a periodic newsletter. Some groups are open; some have membership restrictions (via password).

Listerver discussion groups are also referred to as electronic mailing groups, or, just to confuse matters, mailing lists. Alternatively, they are labeled by reference to the computer managing the group: listservers.

Two warnings are in order. First, you must carefully distinguish between the address of the server that administers the distribution of messages (usually in the form *listserv@address*) and the address of the discussion group to which you send contributions (usually in the form *groupname@address*).

Secondly, provocative news items can trigger a deluge of comments from an ever-increasing membership. Since each subscriber receives all correspondence, hundreds of letters may suddenly appear in your mailbox!

Finding Mailing Lists and Discussion Groups The document "Publicly Accessible Mailing Lists" is posted regularly on the Usenet newsgroup *news.answers*. It is also available by anonymous file transfer protocol (*ftp://rtfm.mit.edu/pub/usenet-by-group/news.answers/mail/mailing-lists*). A listing of listserv groups can be obtained by E-mail from *listserv@ubvm.cc.buffalo.edu* with the message:

**list global */modifier*

where *modifier* indicates a specific search term within newsgroup titles or descriptions.

A number of World Wide Web programs allow you to search publicly accessible mailing lists (and often newsgroups, as well). Some provide hotlinks for obtaining subscriptions or further information (Figure 2).

Liszt: Searchable Directory of E-mail Discussion Groups

http://www.liszt.com/

Mailing Lists WWW Gateway

http://duke.bev.net/cgi-lwgate/lwgate

FIGURE 2   Liszt, a World Wide Web search program for accessing discussion groups that utilize the major listserver programs.

You should, of course, run a number of searches with slightly different search terms to assure that you catch all relevant sites.

Newsgroups

Mailing list and discussion group messages are E-mailed to individual subscribers. With newsgroups, E-mail messages are posted on a variety of independent networks for anyone to read and respond. Primary among these networks is Usenet (User's Network), a large portion of which is carried by the Internet.

Usenet newsgroups provide a forum through which people can gossip, debate, and discuss shared interests, a conferencing system by which people from all walks of life can inform, argue with, query, and harangue each other. Newsgroups are often used to distribute the latest versions of FAQs relating to popular software or any other interest area.

Seven categories of newsgroup postings are distributed worldwide: *news, soc, talk, misc, sci, comp,* and *rec.* There is also an *alt* category, a miscellaneous heading for anything that does not fit elsewhere, and *biz* for business-related groups. In addition, there are subcategories that are limited to a specific institution or geographic area, as well as specialized newsgroup feeds such as the news service ClariNet, the BioNet network, and the history mailing list H–Net. Some such networks combine mailing lists and newsgroups. All messages are both sent to subscribers via E–mail and posted on the appropriate newsgroup.

New users should consult the FAQ posted in *news.announce.newusers* or visit the World Wide Web Usenet Info Center site (*http://sunsite.unc.edu/usenet-i/*).

Using Newsgroups Each newsgroup contains collections of postings or articles that are essentially E-mail messages. Postings on the same topic are assembled into threads.

A special newsreader program is required to read and respond to the postings. Such a reader (the program, that is) typically allows users to subscribe to a specific set of groups from a list of three to four thousand available on any single network. Other newsgroups can still be retrieved, but the system does not have to load all of the messages when starting.

Newsreaders indicate the number of new articles available in each subscribed group. You can save or print a file, search for a particular term, mark files as read, go to the next article in a thread of responses, or respond directly to the author of an article with a new posting (Figure 3).

All newsgroup files are in text mode; graphics and sound files must be decoded prior to viewing.

Finding Newsgroups The search program eXcite (*http://www.excite.com*) can be used to search Usenet groups by keyword or concept. Dejanews (*http://www.dejanews.com/forms/dnq.html*) searches the text of Usenet archives. The Usenet Info Center, cited above, also offers browsing and searching capabilities for Usenet groups.

Social Considerations Usenet groups are at once the essence and the bane of the Internet. Of all sites on the Internet, newsgroups are the preferred venue for uninhibited surfing and lurking (technical terms for scanning and reading without responding). The level of discussion can vary from the intellectual to the puerile, from mainstream to radical. While some newsgroups are moderated for content, discussion is generally uncensored, encouraging a range of belief and expression with which many are uncomfortable. As the forum for the freest expression on the Internet, newsgroups are often subject to restrictions or outright censorship.

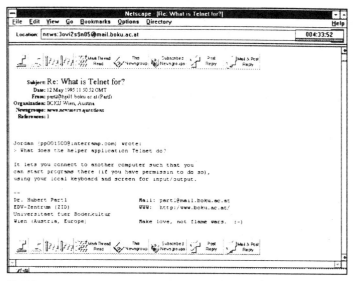

FIGURE 3 A newsgroup posting viewed with the newsreader built into the World Wide Web browser Netscape. Note the command options at the top and bottom of the screen.

Since the anonymity of Internet communication can give rise to relatively antisocial behavior, guides to Internet etiquette ("netiquette") outline traditions of acceptable behavior, such as posting a message to only one newsgroup at a time. Chuq Von Rospach's "A Primer on How to Work with the Usenet Community," a guide to using Usenet politely and efficiently, is available at *news.newusers.questions*. Arlene Rinaldi's "The Net: User Guidelines and Netiquette" is available at *http://rs6000.adm.fau.edu/rinaldi/net/index.htm*.

Talk and Chat Programs

Two other Internet communication programs do not rely on E-mail, but are somewhat simliar in their effect. Talk programs allow two people to "talk" by typing remarks back and forth without exiting their screens. They offer text-based on-line communication.

Chat programs are simply group talk programs. They work somewhat like citizens band radio. Participants can often choose from a list of available chat groups. They can enter or exit a discussion at will, identified only by a handle or nickname they have selected.

Using Talk and Chat Programs Internet talk programs can be initiated at the provider prompt with a **talk** command and an E-mail address. The recipient, assuming he or she is on-line at the time, receives an on-screen message indicating that a session has been initiated. The recipient has only to respond with the same command and the appropriate return E-mail address. A newer program, ntalk ("new talk," of course), is also available.

The Internet version of a chat program, Internet Relay Chat (IRC), requires special software. (For further information, see the newsgroup: *alt.irc*)

New chat programs reflect the general evolution of the Internet toward increasingly sophisticated audio and graphics programs–and with that, a requirement for faster and faster computers, modems, and sound boards. Worlds Chat (*http://www.worlds.net/*) provides a virtual three-dimensional room with photographs of the participants, and Global Chat (*http://www.qdeck.com/chat/globalstage/servers.html*) adds both sound and graphics to an otherwise text-based chat session.

Add real-time voice and chat programs mimic telephones. Internet Phone (*http://www.vocaltec.com*) enables real-time voice conversations between two people. CUSeeMe (*http://cu-seeme.cornell.edu*) allows real-time voice and video conferencing utilizing the Internet.

The Internet Services

4

TELNET: THE INTERNET AS REMOTE CONTROL

Here we begin a survey of the programs available on the Internet. We start with the most general, the plain vanilla operation of simply gaining access to another computer. The program for doing this is called telnet.

Telnet

You can extend the cables of your computer via telephone lines to access the files of a remote computer. The keyboard and screen are your own, but you are "using" another computer.

Remote control of another computer is hardly new with the Internet. You run another computer when you dial up a bulletin board or participate on an office network. What is different with the Internet is the number of activities, and the physical range, available to you.

Many library catalogs, community bulletin boards, and academic and governmental information sites are accessible via telnet. Most of the activities of the Internet can be accomplished by telneting to public access sites.

Using Telnet

As with many Internet terms, the word "telnet" has a number of forms. You use the **telnet** command of the telnet program to telnet to a remote computer.

Upon gaining access to the Internet, simply type the command **telnet** and an address:

prompt% **telnet archie.rutgers.edu**

(Here, as throughout this book, commands and user input are **boldfaced**.) The telnet program contacts the computer at that address using the numerical IP address, waits for a response, and reports its status.

Connected to dorm.Rutgers.EDU.

What happens then depends on where you've telneted to, and the degree to which that site allows public access. As with most other programs, you can obtain a list of possible commands by issuing the command **help** or **?** at the new prompt.

For more information on Telnet, see "Telnet Tips" at *http://galaxy.einet.net/hytelnet/TELNET.html.*

Hytelnet, a database of telnet–accessible sites with appropriate login commands is available by file transfer protocol (*ftp://access.usask.ca/pub/hytelnet*). Alternatively, you can access telnet sites through a search program on the World Wide Web at *http://galaxy.einet.net/hytelnet/HYTELNET.html* (Figure 4).

FILE TRANSFER PROTOCOL AND ARCHIE: THE INTERNET AS LENDING LIBRARY

File Transfer Protocol (FTP)

FTP is a procedure for downloading files from remote computers.

You cannot access any computer, nor can you access everything on a specific computer. The computer in question must be connected to the network and must grant public access to specific directories and activities.

Computers that archive files and grant public access to selected directories are said to offer anonymous file transfer. Roughly three thousand sites provide anonymous FTP service. Two-thirds of these sites are in the United States, and three-fifths of those are located at educational institutions.

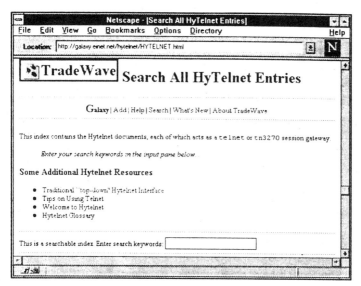

FIGURE 4 A World Wide Web search program for Hytelnet, a catalog of informational sites publically accessible by telnet.

Anonymous FTP archives are an excellent source of Internet software as well as specialized educational and research programs. Documents, position papers, newsletters, photographs, sound files, animated movies, and movie clips are all available by FTP.

Using FTP

FTP servers can be accessed via telnet, from a local FTP host, with graphic-interface programs, or by indicating the URL for an FTP address with a World Wide Web browser. Finally, most documents obtainable via anonymous FTP can be obtained via E-mail.

FTP file retrieval is pursued much as it would be on your own computer. Whatever software program you employ, the sequence is the same:

1. Access the remote computer.

2. Login with a username ("anonymous") and password (by tradition, your E-mail address).

3. Move from subdirectory to subdirectory with change directory (cd) commands to locate the desired file.

4. Read or download the desired file.

5. Repeat steps 3 and 4 as desired.

6. Logoff.

To access an anonymous FTP site with a text-interface program, enter the **ftp** command followed by the address of the desired site at the Internet provider's prompt:

prompt% ftp address-of-FTP-archive

You can access a list of subsequent commands by issuing the command **help** or **?** at the FTP prompt.

With a graphic–interface program or World Wide Web browser, you maneuver through directories by clicking on subdirectory names or icons. You request files by clicking on the filename or icon. Graphic-interface FTP programs usually allow you to maintain a directory of FTP addresses. Simply select an address and the program logs you in and accesses an initial directory (Figure 5).

A complete list of FTP sites generally serves little purpose. We have, after all, little use for a list of all of the libraries in the country; we are more concerned with knowing what books exist and where to find them. Similarly, on the Internet we are more concerned with identifying specific files and their location than with a list of the locations where files might be stored. Nevertheless, a list of Internet sites accepting anonymous FTP is maintained by Perry Rovers at *http://www.info.net/Public/ftp-list.html*.

Instruction in the use of FTP is available in the form of a FAQ document via E-mail from *mail-server@rtfm.mit.edu*. Include no subject and only the message:

send usenet/news.answers/ftp-list/faq

with no final punctuation. You can access FYI 24, How to Use Anonymous FTP (*http://pubweb.nexor.co.uk/public/rfc/rfcs/rfc1635.txt*).

Finally, file transfer from remote computers is not a right. It is a privilege that carries with it distinct responsibilities, such as not downloading files during peak hours. For additional guidance, see the FTP guides above or "The Net: User Guidelines and Netiquette" referred to in the section on newsgroups (page 17).

Archie: The Card Catalog

File transfer protocol provides access to files on computers around the world. But how do you know where to look for a particular file, or for any file of a particular type? You can burrow through the sub-

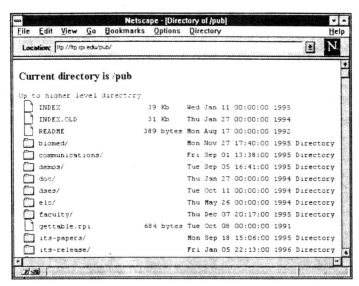

FIGURE 5 A directory listing from an FTP session using the Netscape World Wide Web browser. The options on this screen include returning to the previous level of the directory, displaying text files (indicated by page icons), or proceeding to lower level directories (indicated by file folder icons). The INDEX and README files are generally a useful starting point for any search.

directories and read the indexes on one computer after another, but this is obviously both time consuming and inefficient.

As with other aspects of the Internet, much of your information will come from word of mouth. A magazine article will mention a file. A *read.me* file will refer to another document or program. A newsgroup posting will announce a new program or document. In each case, the address of a relevant FTP server will usually be supplied.

As useful as these resources may be, they will not always suffice. Some means of searching available files is still necessary.

Since the Internet has no center, no central card catalog is possible. A reasonable facsimile, however, is recreated every month at a number of locations by a service and search program called Archie. Sites that offer anonymous FTP register with an Archie service. Over a period of a month, the Archie service scans those sites and generates a list of files and directory names. The resulting database is then mirrored on several other Archie servers, all of which then contain the same information.

Using Archie

Public-access Archie servers are reached by the **telnet** command and a suitable address. Obtain a list of such sites from *telnet://archie.ans.net.* Login as "archie" (all lowercase) and type "servers" at the first prompt. Alternatively, if Archie is installed on your host system, accesss Archie by issuing the **archie** command with no address specified.

Upon reaching an archie server, sign on with the username "archie". No password is necessary. To search for a specific program, type the command **prog** followed by the name of the program. The command **help** or **?** at the archie prompt will list other available commands.

Archie servers often indicate your place in line (queue position) and the expected time of completion of a search. While there are thousands of FTP servers, there are a limited number of Archie servers. A queue position of 35 is not uncommon. If the anticipated delay is long, simply try another server. In most cases, a server will offer a list of other active servers.

As with graphic-interface FTP programs, graphic-interface Archie programs store lists of server addresses and automatically submit the userid "archie" at the login prompt.

Archie searches combined with FTP retrieval are available at various Web sites, including the Archie Request Form at NCSA (*http://hoohoo.ncsa.uiuc.edu/archie.html*) (Figure 6).

GOPHER AND VERONICA: THE INTERNET AS RESEARCH LIBRARY

Gopher

Gopher is a tool for burrowing or tunneling through file resources on the Internet. It is akin to browsing from a document in one library to another document in another library.

Gopher is based on menus. Gopher menus point to other menus, which ultimately point to specific documents, whether text, picture, animation, sound file, or search program on the same or other computers.

While all types of files can be accessed using Gopher, a Gopher screen displays either a menu or a document–no graphics, fancy fonts, or icons. Sound and graphics files must be downloaded for viewing later.

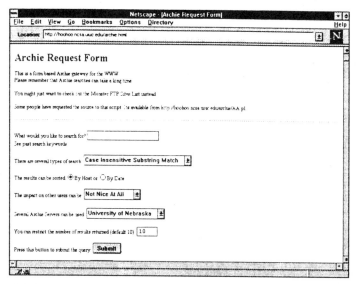

FIGURE 6   A World Wide Web Archie program. Note the search options.

As with other services, you can access only what someone lets you. Gopher sites are for the most part located at academic institutions and government agencies. The resulting materials are therefore of an academic/research/statistical nature. Entertainment, commercial, and lifestyle resources tend to be cataloged on the more recent World Wide Web.

Using Gopher

You can access Gopher menus in various ways.

If your Internet provider offers no Gopher service, you can use the **telnet** command to access any of a dozen or so public-access Gopher sites.

If Gopher service is offered by your Internet provider, the **gopher** command alone accesses the provider's initial menu and the **gopher** command followed by an address reaches a specific Gopher site anywhere in the world.

Finally, you can access specific Gopher sites with specialized graphic-interface programs or a World Wide Web browser.

Since all Gophers provide access to all Gopherspace, you can get to any Gopher from any other.

One of the standard starting points on most systems is a topic-oriented menu called Gopher Jewels. With text–interface, the initial menu looks like this:

Gopher Jewels

1. GOPHER JEWELS Information and Help/
2. Community, Global and Environmental/
3. Education, Social Sciences, Arts & Humanities/
4. Economics, Business and Store Fronts/
5. Engineering and Industrial Applications/
6. Government/
7. Health, Medical, and Disability/
8. Internet and Computer Related Resources/
9. Law/
10. Library, Reference, and News/
11. Miscellaneous Items/
12. Natural Sciences including Mathematics/
13. Personal Development and Recreation/
14. Research, Technology Transfer and Grants Opportunities/
15. Search Gopher Jewels Menus by Key Word(s) <?>

Page: 1/1

Markings at the end of each line indicate the nature of each menu item. A right slash, / , indicates that the item leads to a lower-level menu. The question mark within brackets, < ? > , indicates a searchable database.

Since Gopher is menu-based, text–interface and graphic-interface sessions look pretty much the same (Figure 7).

Negotiating from one Gopher menu to another is accomplished with cursor keys or by clicking on icons. To select a menu item, simply move the cursor to the item and hit the enter key or point and click with a mouse. The Gopher program issues a telnet, FTP, or other command to access that item.

If you reach a dead end, double back to an earlier choice by clicking on an icon representing the earlier menu or, with a text-based system, by hitting the left cursor.

Gopher programs allow you to create a personal menu of your favorite Gopher sites (bookmarks) for later use. The Gopher FAQ is located at *gopher://mudhoney.micro.umn.edu/70/00/gopher.faq*.

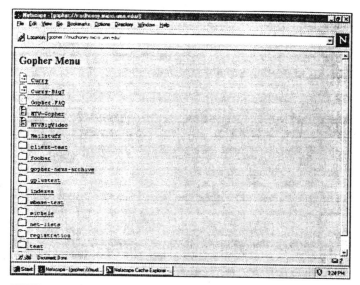

FIGURE 7   Gopher menu viewed with a World Wide Web browser.

In the end, Gopher is essentially a browsing tool. You can pursue material on specific topics, but since you have to hunt around, it is not really a search program. Gopher is also a retrieval program. (You will recall that file transfer protocol was a retrieval program, not really a search tool, and Archie a search tool but not a tool for retrieval.)

The value of Gopher is in great part not only what you find at the end of your travels but what you discover along the way. The investigation itself will often suggest additional topics and resources you may never have imagined.

Veronica: Searching with Gopher

As a browser, Gopher offers a slow and haphazard approach to research. A more direct route is available, however.

Veronica (Very Easy Rodent-Oriented Net-Wide Index to Computerized Archives) builds a searchable index of Gopher menus in much the same way that Archie builds an index of FTP files. Every week, about a dozen Veronica sites search and index the titles in menus of registered Gopher servers. The result is a searchable database of virtually all of the Gopher servers in the world.

Veronica goes one step further. Archie told you where files were; you had to get them yourself using FTP. The output from a Veronica search is a custom Gopher menu. Veronica is thus both a search and a retrieval tool.

Since Veronica is a tool of Gophers, it appears as an option on the initial menu of most Gopher servers. There is no need for a **veronica** command. If one of the Veronica indexes is unavailable due to high traffic, simply try another (Figure 8). The home base for Veronica is at *gopher://veronica.scs.unr.edu/11/veronica*.

Jughead (Jonzy's Universal Gopher Hierarchy Excavation and Display), a variant of Veronica, searches file names and directories on a select number of Gophers or the immediate Gopher server.

Using Veronica

Veronica searches menus, not the contents of the Gopher servers themselves. Veronica indexes do, however, include additional items, such as titles from World Wide Web servers, Usenet archives, and telnet information services that are referenced on Gopher menus.

Veronica searches are not case-sensitive (searching for Tuba will locate TUBA, tuba, and Tuba), and Veronica understands the Boolean logical operators AND, NOT, OR (a blank is assumed to be AND). Additional commands allow you to restrict the search to certain types of files or a maximum number of responses. Veronica also supports partial word searches in which an asterisk "*" represents a wild card character or characters. "Go*" will return all items that have a word beginning with "go" in the title.

Veronica search terms will appear in every menu item. This is as it should be; after all, searches are defined as searches for specific words in menu titles. But such a search will obviously fail to include closely associated items or similar items described in different terms.

Here, as in all research, there is a distinct art to selecting the proper search terms. Try alternate searches using synonyms or more general terms to assure yourself that you are capturing all of the relevant references. If a search yields an inordinate number of responses, search again with a more limited search term. If you desire more options, search again with an alternative phrase or more general terms, or browse some of the sites indicated and see what you find.

When you know exactly what term or phrase best describes what you are looking for, a Veronica search can be more direct–and potentially more fruitful–than simply following Gopher menus.

For an extended discussion of Veronica search techniques, see the FAQ document "how-to-query-veronica" offered with Veronica menus.

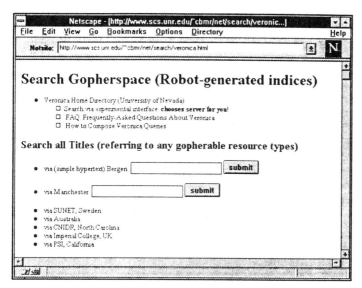

FIGURE 8 A World Wide Web Veronica interface.

WAIS: SEARCHING DOCUMENTS

WAIS

Archie searches file names in directories of anonymous FTP servers; Veronica searches key words in Gopher menus. Neither examines documents themselves, only their listing in a directory or menu. WAIS (pronounced "waze"), on the other hand, is specifically document oriented.

The WAIS (Wide Area Information Servers) information retrieval system on the Internet is an application of a more general search protocol. WAIS examines the full text of all of the documents on a particular database. It searches for key words and ranks documents according to the number and placement of the "hits." Like Veronica, WAIS offers a menu from which you can then retrieve documents.

In actual fact, WAIS searches not documents but *indexes* of the text of documents. As a result, the WAIS database can include anything that can be indexed with words. Descriptions of insects or works of art can be indexed to pictures of the items. Descriptions of songs can be indexed to sound files. In the end, however, you can only access what has been indexed.

There are roughly six hundred free public databases, each devoted to a particular collection of materials, each with the *.src* extension indicating a WAIS database.

WAIS databases exist for newsgroups, professional journals, and bibliographies. They include databases of Hubble Space Telescope Instrument Status Reports, U.S. Department of Agriculture commodity market reports, and the Columbia Law School card catalogue. Fewer WAIS databases exist for nonacademic areas or for topics for which the relevant materials are widely dispersed.

Using WAIS

WAIS can be accessed by the telnet command at *quake.think.com* (login as "wais") or at a number of other public-access sites, as an option on some Gopher menus, or via the World Wide Web (*http://www.ai.mit.edu/the-net/wais.html*) (Figure 9). It can also be accessed by E-mail at *WAISmail@quake.think.com*. (Here again, the message "help" will elicit a list of the proper commands.)

A WAIS search involves a number of steps:

1. Select the appropriate database(s) (sources)
2. Select key-word search term(s) (questions)
3. Indicate the maximum number of responses desired
4. Search the specific database(s)
5. Review the results and access specific files

If you do not know which database to search, you can first search a directory of servers, *directory-of-servers.scr*, and then select appropriate databases from the initial output (Figure 10).

As with Veronica searches, WAIS searches must be executed with care. A single word can have different meanings in different contexts. You must, then, decide how relevant the resulting hits actually are, and re-search if necessary.

A search on the word "table," for instance, would locate references to furniture (kitchen table), economic charts (statistical tables), and parliamentary procedure (table a motion). To be more specific in your search, you might search on additional terms that are likely to occur in the same context. Alternatively, newer WAIS programs allow for relevance checking, a means of refining a second search based on the results of the first. Newer programs also allow the use of Boolean logic in search terms.

Above all, you must be careful not to assume that a lack of citations necessarily implies a lack of evidence. It may be that you just didn't look as imaginatively as you might have.

WAIS is most suitable when you are looking for unspecified information related to a very specific term or are searching a select

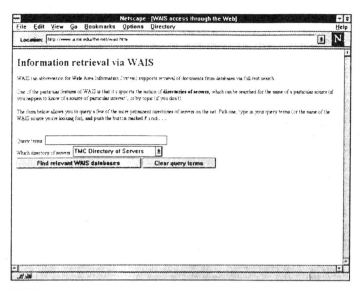

FIGURE 9 A World Wide Web site offering access to WAIS searches.

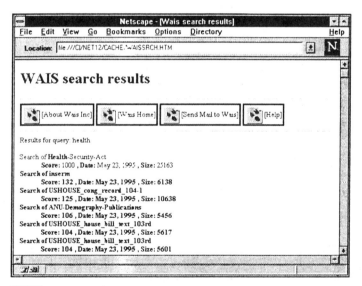

FIGURE 10 Initial WAIS search results searching on the question "health" in the *directory-of-servers.src* database, listed by score.

database for known information. If you want to find out about the American welfare system, Gopher or the World Wide Web would be a more appropriate resource. The WAIS FAQ is available at *http://www.uoknor.edu/research/electron/internet/wais-faq.htm.* It should be noted, however, that this service has been superceded by World Wide Web pages and increasingly complex World Wide Web search programs.

THE WORLD WIDE WEB: THE INTERNET AS MULTIMEDIA

Of all the aspects of the Internet, the World Wide Web (WWW) has evoked the greatest hyperbole. Laurie Flynn, in *The New York Times,* referred to it as "an electronic amalgam of the public library, the suburban shopping mall and the Congressional Record," while Peter H. Lewis, in the same newspaper, referred to it as "a time-sucking black hole... a speedtrap on the data highway, a Bermuda Triangle in the information ocean, the junk food aisle in cyberspace's digital supermarket."

The Web, as it is often called, is the fastest growing service on the Internet. In just a few years, it has become an integral, and for some indispensable, part of the culture.

As with Gopher, the World Wide Web is a means of accessing files on computers connected via the Internet. The World Wide Web is not a physical place, nor a set of files, nor even a network of computers. The heart of the World Wide Web lies in the protocols that define its use. Yet it is the appearance of the Web that is most striking.

The Look!

Each Web site opens with a home page, "a combination frontispiece, greeting room, table of contents, hub, and launching pad," in the words of Michael Neubarth, editor-in-chief of *Internet World.*

Gopher menus can lead to files that contain pictures or sound or even movie clips, but the overall presentation of the menus is text. A typical Gopher menu, even viewed with a graphics program, still looks like a menu of items (Figure 7). The World Wide Web, on the other hand, is the only truly multimedia presentation on the Internet. You have only to look at a World Wide Web screen to see the difference (Figure 11)!

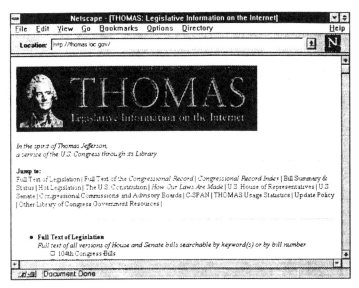

FIGURE 11   Thomas World Wide Web home page utilizing graphics.

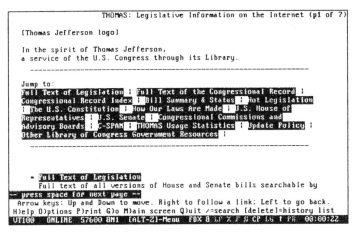

FIGURE 12   Thomas World Wide Web page viewed with the text-
interface browser Lynx. Note the indication of the number
of screens for the complete page at the top.

A Web page has all of the aspects of sophisticated desktop publishing: diverse typefaces, charts and forms, icons and integrated
graphics. Sound and movies can even be integrated into the presentation. Recent increases in computer speed have spawned applications utilizing real-time sound and 3-D or virtual reality graphics.

To be sure, the World Wide Web can be accessed with a text interface, but it has none of the panache of the graphics version. Elements that appear highlighted by color in a graphic interface appear as underlined or shadowed text (Figure 12).

What's Behind It All: Hypertext

The World Wide Web is based on the notion of links within hypertext pages.

In hypertext, key concepts and ideas are linked to the address of related material, in much the same manner that each item in a Gopher menu is encoded with the location of the requisite menu or file. Links within the discussion are indicated by highlighted terms, icons, or simply locations on the page called hotspots. Click on a hotspot, and you access the linked item, be it another Web page or any one of a number of the other Internet services. Footnote numbers can provide direct access to the original sources. Links can be inserted into maps and drawings. You can click on a room in a blueprint and see a photograph of that room.

The overall effect is not unlike reading an encyclopedia with the ability to snap your fingers to instantly shift to another page, another book, or even a phonograph or slide projector! You do not need to follow a predetermined sequence of ideas. You can branch off as your interests dictate.

Hypertext Transfer Protocol (HTTP)

Hypertext linkage is accomplished with Hypertext Transfer Protocol (HTTP), the main operating system of the World Wide Web–hence the URL notation *http://*. This protocol contains the instructions to connect to a remote computer, request a specified document, receive the document, and sever the connection.

Hypertext Markup Language (HTML)

The coding of a World Wide Web page is done with Hypertext Markup Language (HTML). Just as a word processor inserts codes to indicate fonts and font sizes, paragraph breaks and boldface, so HTML inserts tags or elements to accomplish the same effects. The resulting format is seen only when the page is read by a Web browser.

The following is the HTML document underlying the Thomas home page. Addresses are indicated in universal resource locator

(URL) notation. On-screen text has been marked in boldface to distinguish it from the hypertext markup language coding. Hyperlinks, indicated on screen by a contrasting color, are indicated here in italics.

<!doctype html public "-//W3O//DTD WWW HTML 2.0//EN">
<HTML>
<HEAD>
<TITLE>**THOMAS: Legislative Information on the Internet**</TITLE>
<!BASE HREF="http://thomas.loc.gov/home/thomas.html">
</HEAD>
<BODY>
<img src= "http://thomas.loc.gov/home/thom_mas.gif"
alt="[Thomas
Jefferson logo] ">
<P><EM>**In the spirit of Thomas Jefferson,**
a service of the U.S. Congress through its Library.</EM>
<HR>
<STRONG>**Jump to:**</STRONG>
<A HREF="#legislation">*Full Text of Legislation*</A> |
<A HREF="#record">*Full Text of the*<I>*Congressional Record*</I></A> |
<A HREF="#index"><I>*Congressional Record Index*</I></A> |
<A HREF="#bss">*Bill Summary & Status*</A> |
<A HREF="#hot">*Hot Legislation*</A> |
<A HREF="http://lcweb2.loc.gov:8080/constquery.html">*The U.S. Constitution*</A> |
<A HREF="http://thomas.loc.gov/home/lawsmade.toc.html">
<I>*How Our Laws Are Made*</I></A> |
<A HREF="#house">*U.S. House of Representatives*</A> |
<A HREF="#senate">*U.S. Senate*</A> |
<A HREF="#congcom">*Congressional Commissions and Advisory Boards*</A> |
<A HREF="#cspan">*C-SPAN*</A> |
<A HREF = "http://thomas.loc.gov/stats/stats.html">*THOMAS Usage Statistics*</A> |
<A HREF="#update">*Update Policy*</A> |
<A HREF="#resources">*Other Library of Congress Government Resources*</A> |</P> <HR>
<UL>
<P>
<LI><A NAME="legislation"><STRONG>**Full Text of Legislation**</STRONG></A>

<EM>**Full text of all versions of House and Senate bills searchable by keyword(s) or by bill number.**</EM>
<UL>
<LI><a href="http://thomas.loc.gov/home/c104query.html">*104th Congress Bills*</a>

....

Notice that an HTML document, unlike a document produced with a word processor, is in plain ASCII text. The result is a universally accessible page that can be read by browsers using any operating system, whether Windows, Macintosh, or UNIX.

For discussion of Hypertext Markup Language, see A Beginner's Guide to HTML (*http://www.ncsa.uiuc.edu/General/Internet/ WWW/HTMLPrimer.html*), HTML Help (*http://www.obscure.org/ ~jaws/htmlhelp.html*), or The Almost Complete HTML Reference (*http://www.hawaiian.net/~wired/htmlref/*).

Web Browsers

The World Wide Web is accessed with programs called browsers. The browser Mosaic is to a great extent responsible for the initial explosion of the World Wide Web; Netscape has since become the standard for most users, and is responsible for the continuing expansion.

A Web browser is in reality an HTML reader. A browser reads the HTML code indicating such attributes as bold <STRONG>, a list of items <LI>, or links <A HREF=>. Not all browsers can decode newer codes, such as those for background colors or user–input forms; and users can control some attributes, such as the size and font of the type. Thus, while all browsers can read any HTML page, any single page can look different on different browsers.

Web browsers open on a default home page. It may be the home page of your provider, the home page of the browser program, or any page that you have designated. Utilizing Hypertext Transfer Protocol, Web browsers access Web locations, follow hypertext links, and create an ongoing history of the sites visited in your travels.

Using the World Wide Web

Text-based browsers such as Lynx can be launched from public-access sites using the **telnet** command or as selections on the higher-level menus of many Gophers. Alternatively, access with

Lynx is available directly from a provider prompt. Simply type **lynx** followed by a Web address expressed in URL format:

prompt% **lynx http://thomas.loc.gov**

The command **lynx**, alone, accesses the default home page of your Internet provider.

Graphic-interface programs such as Mosaic or Netscape follow essentially the same process. Simply enter an appropriate address (or use the default site) and click on highlighted terms or icons to move from site to site. No fancy commands are necessary.

If you have used that browser before, you will have saved a list of bookmarks or hotlinks leading to your favorite sites. Alternatively, you can start from one of a number of menus, indexes, or key-word search programs.

The World Wide Web FAQ, offering discussion on both World Wide Web resources and browsers, is located at *http://www.boutell.com/faq/www_faq.html.*

The Glory and the Hype

The attention given the World Wide Web is in huge part deserved— but only in part.

Due to the added space required by fancy fonts and graphics, the text of most hypertext displays on the World Wide Web is decidedly cursory. The full opportunity for lengthy discussion is rarely taken. You find, instead, essentially an illustrated and annotated menu. Whereas a Gopher menu might offer 15 possible paths on a single screen, the opening screen of a Web site often has no more than 5 links, if that many. While many Gopher menus are complete on a single screen, a full view of most Web pages requires scanning a number of screens. These problems are clearly due in part to a lack of sophistication in writing Web pages, but the problems remain.

Content is also an issue. Many corporate home pages offer the electronic equivalent of junk mail, filled with what Bart Zeigler of the *Wall Street Journal* has descibed as "turgid company profiles, hokey product pitches and bland marketing material... that wouldn't make it from the mailbox to the kitchen counter of most homes if they arrived via the Postal Service."

Speed is another consideration. You pay for graphics with reduced speed. The text version of the opening page of the Thomas Congressional site uses 7,838 bytes of information. The opening graphic alone is another 31,280 bytes. In short, the screen with full graphics takes at least five times as long to receive. With a 14,400-baud modem, the

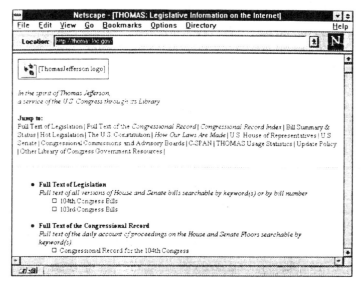

FIGURE 13   Thomas World Wide Web home page without graphics.

wait is annoying and at times seems interminable. The delay with animation, sound messages, or movies is even more profound. In response to this problem, new browsers load the text first, painting in pictures later, or allow you to view the screen in a text format with pictures replaced by icons (Figure 13).

Finally, anyone on the Internet can establish a home page presence on the Web. There is no committee to go through, no certification to acquire, no large investment in hardware required. Many Internet providers and on-line services now offer this opportunity to their subscribers.

The ease with which Web sites can be established has both advantages and disadvantages. On the one hand, it guarantees openness and diversity. On the other hand, the Web is subject to an overabundance of choices, many of questionable value. With broader access to the Web via on-line services, the increase in new sites has been accelerated by businesses anticipating methods for secure credit card transactions on the Internet.

Even with all the problems, in many instances the resources of the Web are without equal. For maps, product pictures, photographs, artwork, and other illustrative material, there is no substitute.

Constructing Your Own Home Page

Anyone can create a home page to use as an opening page with
their browser. No programming experience is required. For help
making a home page you can read Dr. Randall Hansen's Web Publishing Resources (*http://www.stetson.edu/~hansen/web.html*), or complete the forms at the Home Page Generator (*http://www.interline.net/
HomePage.htm*).

Writing home pages is relatively simple. Getting a home page
on the Internet is another matter. The easiest approach is to find a
server that will carry your home page—either at your university or
through your Internet service provider.

Research on the Internet 5

GENERAL CONCERNS

What am I looking for, and where can I find it? Research is

- initiated by questions,
- guided by knowledge and reflection, and
- driven by feedback.

All of which is to say that much of research is a matter of trial and error. But it is a methodical and informed trial and error.

Research Is Initiated by Questions

Research begins with questions, with wanting to know something. You may seek specific information about a specific topic (What is the atomic weight of uranium?) or a wide range of ideas on a broad topic (How might welfare be revised?). One way or another, you want to know something you don't already know.

If you think you know it all, there is no need for research. If you want to see if you're right, that is in itself a question and a legitimate basis for research.

Finally, research assumes that the information you want to know exists, and that it is available where you can find it. The real question, then, is where to look. Or even more to the point, how to find out where to look. Which brings us to the second point.

Research Is Guided by Knowledge and Reflection

The more you know about what you want to find, the easier it is to find it. This may seem obvious, but it is also profound. Without prior reflection, you can waste hours chasing inappropriate sources, hours that could be saved with a little thought before you started. In what context does a term appear? Surely that will provide a start. Alternatively, you might ask: Who cares? Who would want to know? If you know who cares about a topic or issue, you are well along the way to finding out who might collect information, store it, and have it available.

Here, as elsewhere, research requires that you generalize, that you recognize the *kind* of thing you are dealing with, that you classify or categorize ideas.

Different kinds of information will, obviously, be found in different places. Without knowing *something* about what you are looking for, you cannot even start! Once you recognize the kind of information you are seeking, you are well on your way to realizing where it might be found.

Research Is Driven by Feedback

Research is a matter of discovery, discrimination, and elimination. Everything you find, or do not find, shapes your further inquiry.

If you find what you want, well and good. If you don't, the trick is to turn momentary failure into a productive learning experience.

The discovery of the *absence* of data is often as important as discovery of relevant data itself. You must determine if nothing is there or whether you just didn't find it. If not here, then where? Try alternate search strategies to assure that information is truly unavailable.

As you search, you will discover new interests or topics. As you eliminate one source, you will be led to others.

INTERNET CONCERNS

The resources of the Internet are indeed enormous and ever expanding. Resources unheard of only a few years ago are now commonplace. But, as we suggested, you must first have some idea of what's out there, and know how to find what you want when you want it.

Know Your Options

Knowing *where* to look depends greatly on knowing where you *might* look. You should be aware of the existence of, and uses of, a number of electronic resources–both in general and in your field of interest, such as:

databases (both public and commercial)

abstract services

specialized on-line library collections

professional associations

state and government agencies

nonprofit organizations

usenet newsgroups and listerver discussion groups

anonymous FTP software archives

Know How to Get What You Want

Knowing what is on the Internet, and where it is, is only half the story. You also have to know how to get where you want to go. You must understand the variety of services and the programs necessary to access those services.

To use the services effectively, you should understand how each service organizes and accesses information. That means such things as knowing the addresses of gopher subject menus and why you might choose to use Veronica instead of a World Wide Web search program. It means knowing whether a particular search program accepts Boolean logic in its search terms and how to properly formulate such searches.

To use the Internet–and your own time–effectively, you must distinguish between active discovery and idle diversion, between productive research and sheer busywork.

Authorship, Authenticity, Authoritativeness, and Value

When you pick up a book or newspaper, you have a certain confidence in the authenticity of the material. Examining a book or professional journal in a library, you are aware that it has been selected from among competing texts and reviewed by an editor prior to publication, and selected from among competing publications by a librarian for inclusion in the collection. The title and copyright page attest to the true author and place and date of publication. And you are reasonably certain the document exists in the form intended by the author. With the Internet, all of these assumptions may fall under suspicion. When it is easy to create personnae, it is hard to verify credentials. Internet citations have no page numbers or publication dates, and a reader pursuing a citation may find the text has been moved or altered—with no way to know the difference.

On the whole, Internet data is no more authoritative than any other—and in many cases less so. While we may delight in the fact that we can post anything we want on sections of the Internet, when we are looking for information we would like to be able to distinguish beforehand between a professor's treatise and Jonny's seventh grade school report. "Anyone who has attempted to obtain information from the internet," an editorial in the *Journal of Chemical Education* observed, "knows that you are as likely to find garbage as you are to find quality information." The affiliation of a server may suggest a certain degree of reliability, but that in itself should indicate neither approval nor review by anyone else at that institution.

While the Internet may have the richness and range of a world-class encyclopedia, that does not mean you want to, or need to, read every article. Much of the current material on the Internet is outdated or only offers snippets of information. Much of the discussion on newsgroups is simply chatter. Just because you can download thousands of files does not mean you need any of them.

One the bright side, since it is easier to publish material on the Internet than it is to publish books, information available on the Internet is often more up-to-date than information in printed texts. But that is useful only for information that changes frequently, or has changed recently.

INTERNET TACTICS AND STRATEGIES

Is the Internet the Best Tool to Use?

You may turn to the Internet to save time, to save effort, or to find better sources of information. But just because you have access to the Internet does not mean the Internet is necessarily the best tool for a particular project. Many times, other procedures are quicker, easier, and more certain to yield results.

Try the Obvious First

The general rule should be: Try the obvious first. This seems self evident, but it often needs restating. To find the Latin name for lions you can turn on your computer, logon to your Internet service, access a search program, input a search term, wait for a response, evaluate the sources provided, and continue on to a specific location. Or you can flip open a collegiate dictionary and look it up. There's a lesson there.

Networking for Knowledge

The car manufacturer Packard long ago had a slogan: Ask the man who owns one. With research: Ask someone who knows. You can use E-mail to communicate with others, or check archives of frequently asked questions of a relevant newsgroup. You can participate in the communication of a discussion group.

Overall, however, you are more likely to gain fresh insights and understanding through the interchange of talking to someone else than you are punching keys on a keyboard and staring at a computer screen.

What You Can, and Cannot, Find

The Internet was developed for scientists to exchange data and ideas. While much of the emphasis has shifted to commercial and entertainment applications, the Internet remains a vital link in academic and scientific communication.

In recent years governmental agencies at all levels have made increasing amounts of information available on the Internet. Many professional associations and interest groups maintain home pages on the World Wide Web.

Still, no one gives anything of value away for free. While you can access some encyclopedias on the Internet, the premiere volume, *Encyclopedia Britannica*, is available only by commercial subscription.

Full texts of professional journals are, for the most part, available only in hard copy. Nevertheless, journals increasingly offer tables of contents, archives of abstracts, and supplemental tables, illustrations, or data, as well as searchable indexes of past issues on the Internet.

Commercial full-text databases such as Nexis/Lexis and Dialog can often be accessed via the Internet for a fee. Students and faculty, however, often have access to such proprietary databases on-line or on CD-ROM in college libraries.

Selecting an Appropriate Service

Each service of the Internet accesses different resources. Each is, therefore, useful for different purposes. Which you turn to will depend on what you are looking for.

E-mail

If you wish to contact **specific people,** or **post a message to a discussion group or newsgroup,** E-mail is the program to use.

Listserv / Discussion Groups

If wish to locate **individuals as representatives of an organization or sharing a specific interest,** listserv discussion groups may be appropriate.

Newsgroups

If you seek **current discussion of a particular topic or issue,** or **to identify individuals with a specific interest,** newsgroups are the desired choice.

FTP/Archie

If you seek **specific computer files,** especially programs related to the Internet, file transfer protocol would be the obvious starting point. If you are not sure where to find specific files, the associated search program, Archie, is a useful tool.

Gopher/Veronica

If you wish to locate **documents, files, information, or data from or about a specific education, governmental or nonprofit organization or association,** you might check to see if they (or anyone else) have a Gopher server with the desired resources. The search program Veronica can be of service here, as well as for just about any academic, governmental, or computer-related topic.

WAIS

If you are seeking **specific documents** or the content of a certain type of document or database, WAIS, the sole program aimed at full-text searches would be in order.

World Wide Web

If you wish to locate **documents, files, information, or data from or about a specific business or commercial enterprise,** the World Wide Web would be the most direct source. The same is true for **product information and technical**

assistance. And the Web is the choice for most **multimedia presentations,** whether sound, movies, or simply graphics, as well as for the **site of home pages for popular issues and concerns.**

Finally, remember that many World Wide Web search programs include references to other aspects of the Internet, and often even provide direct links to them.

Budgeting Your Time and On-line Time

The general rule for efficient use of the Internet is simple: logon, get what you want, and logoff.

You want to know what you're looking for beforehand and have a plan for accessing it. You want to get the information you seek, and get out. This is especially true when you are incurring hourly expenses imposed by on-line services and Internet providers.

You can save time and money by downloading information for later perusal. Off-line time is cheaper than on-line time, and hard copies are easier to read than text on screens.

Both text and graphic-interface programs offer some means of automatically capturing on-screen text during a session. You can save hypertext pages on the World Wide Web in a cache directory for closer examination off-line.

Spend your time on-line evaluating information, not looking up addresses. If your software program allows it, maintain directories of sites for FTP, Gopher, and WAIS programs. If this is not possible, keep a log of addresses handy. When using Gopher and World Wide Web programs, make bookmarks for sites you return to often.

Citations and Plagiarism

You can save time and effort by downloading documents instead of finding published texts and photocopying them. You can then insert that text directly into your own writing.

While a great convenience, this process has obvious dangers. You can confuse your text with text that you have downloaded, and in so doing commit the crime of plagiarism. And you can lose track of information for proper citations.

To avoid plagiarism, store downloaded text with a special font–such as *italic* or SMALL CAPITAL LETTERS–and change the font only when the material has been properly cited within your discussion.

The address of Internet documents is often equivalent to the publication data associated with books. While no standards have been universally accepted, tentative standards are discussed at *http://www.cas.usf.edu/english/walker/mla.html.*

INTERNET RESEARCH RESOURCES

As with all research, research on the Internet has to start somewhere. Once you know what you are looking for, you have to select tools to work with.

Browsing versus Searching

There are essentially two approaches to research on the Internet: browsing and searching.

Gopher and the World Wide Web menus offer choices for browsing. Archie, Veronica, WAIS, and various World Wide Web search programs offer key-word search opportunities that, in the latter two cases, then offer initial menus for browsing.

Searching begins with selecting a search program or engine and a search term or terms. Browsing requires, once again, a choice of where to start browsing.

Desk Reference Tools

We might start with menus that offer, in effect, electronic versions of standard library resources such as the U.S. Geographic Names Database, U.S. Telephone Area Codes, Webster's Dictionary, the CIA World Fact Book, or headlines from the Associated Press/Reuters News Wire Service.

Many universities offer menus of basic desk reference tools on Gopher or the World Wide Web. See Reference Resources via the World Wide Web (*http://vm.cfsan.fda.gov/referenc.html*) or access desk reference tools at:

The Virtual Reference Desk at Purdue University

http://thorplus.lib.purdue.edu/reference/index.html

Indiana State

gopher://odin.indstate.edu:70/11/ref.dir/info.dir

National Institute of Health

gopher://odie.niaid.nih.gov:70/11/deskref

Desk reference menus can offer a useful starting point for browsing.

Comprehensive Subject Guides

Comprehensive subject guides, such as the following, are excellent
candidates as bookmarks for your browser program.

Gopher Jewels

http://galaxy.einet.net/GJ/index.html

Special Internet Connections, by Scott Yanoff

http://www.spectracom.com/islist

An extensive list of specific sites under academic and
general headings

YAHOO (Yet Another Hierarchically Odiferous Oracle)

http://www.yahoo.com

A convenient and extensive subject-area listing of World
Wide Web sites, plus a search tool

Government Information Locator Service (GILS)

http://info.er.usgs.gov/gils/index.html

The best resource list, of course, is the one *you* develop from your
own experience to meet your own needs.

Discipline-Specific Guides

Every discipline has specialized resources. The Clearinghouse for
Subject-Oriented Internet Resource Guides, a joint effort of the University of Michigan's University Library and School of Information
and Library Studies, offers guides to resources on the Internet for
roughly 200 subject areas, from statistics to women's health resources, job hunting to alternative medicine. A Gopher version
(*gopher://gopher.lib.umich.edu*) and a slightly abridged hypertext
version (*http://www.clearinghouse.net*) are available. The guides
often run 20 to 30 pages.

Alternatively, you can create your own discipline-specific guide
by running a search program on a general topic, as you might with
a Yahoo search on biology

http://www.yahoo.com/Science/Biology

Guides such as these can be invaluable sources of addresses, as well
as of clickable links, for further investigation.

Key-Word Search Programs

When you have no idea where to start, you might turn to a key-word search program. This solution, however, is not as surefire as it might first appear.

Key-word search programs are useful for finding unique names of persons or places (proper nouns) or specific terminology for which there would be no likely synonym. They are not as useful for general terms for which there might be a plethora of resources.

Once you decide that a key-word search is appropriate, other decisions must be made. You must choose a particular search program and, with that, what to search and how.

Major key-word search programs include:

eXcite

http://www.excite.com

DEC AltaVista

http://www.altavista.digital.com

Yahoo Search

http://www.yahoo.com

Lycos Search

http://lycos.cs.cmu.edu

New search programs are constantly appearing. An up-to-date list can always be obtained at *http://www.yahoo.com/ computers_and_internet/internet/world_wide_web/searching _the_web/ search_Engines/* or *http://rs.internic.net/scout/toolkit/search.html.*

No single search program searches all of the Internet. Different search programs search different databases, or search the same ones differently. Some search titles or headers of documents, others search the documents themselves, still others search other indexes or directories. Some search the URLs describing the location of a text, others the URLs embedded within hypertext pages. Finally, some search programs also search other databases, such as Gopher listings. (See "Web search tool features," *http://www.unn.ac.uk/ features.htm* and Understanding WWW Search Tools, *http://www.indiana.edu/~librcsd/search/*)

Sites such as the MetaCrawler Multi-Threaded Web Search Service (*http://metacrawler.cs.washington.edu:8080/index.html*) offer simultaneous searching of a variety of search programs, while sites such as RES-Links: The All-in-One Resource Page (*http://www.cam.org/~intsci/*) offer links to a wide variety of search engines covering all aspects of the Internet, not only the World Wide Web.

The sheer number of citations returned need not be the major concern. A large number of "hits" from mailing list correspondence may not be that productive. Again, your research must be guided by knowledge and reflection.

Glossary

Anonymous FTP   A file retrieval program with a common public password. *See also* File Transfer Protocol.

Archie   A search program providing listings of the locations of files available by anonymous FTP. Also the automated indexing program upon which such searches are based.

Archive (verb)   To combine two or more files into one.

Archive site   A computer that stores and provides access to a specific collection of files.

ASCII file   A file encoding format, developed by the American Standard Code for Information Interchange, that represents upper- and lowercase letters, numbers, punctuation marks, and basic operations (for example, tab, enter) by numbers from 1 to 128. A file encoded in standard keyboard characters—as opposed to a binary file. An unformatted text file. *See also* Binary file.

Binary   Represented by ones and zeros, for example, 11001001.

Binary file   A file encoded in binary code. More often, a file encoded with characters including but not limited to those found on a standard keyboard. Executable programs are stored as binary or nontext files.

Bit (binary digit)   A single unit of data.

Browser Specifically, a program for reading the Hypertext Markup Language of World Wide Web pages. More generally, any program for following a path of menu items or other links.

Bulletin board system (BBS) An on-line computer network offering information and messages. Generally nonprofit and local or interest-group focused. *See also* On-line service.

Byte Eight bits. The number of bits necessary to indicate a single number or letter of the alphabet.

Chat A program or forum for on-line group discussion.

Client A computer system, program, or user that requests services from another computer, the server, on a network. *See also* Server.

Compression The reduction in the size of a file to achieve a smaller storage space or faster transmission.

Cyberspace The electronic world of computers and their users. The conglomerate information and resources of the Internet and other networked communication services.

Database Any collection of data or interrelated files that can be accessed in a variety of ways.

Decode To convert an encoded file back to its original form. *See also* Encode.

Digital Generally, using numbers or other discrete units–as with a digital, as opposed to analog, watch. The term is synonymous with any binary–coded system or device, hence essentially synonymous with *computer*.

Directory An index of the location of files, as on a hard drive of a computer. Directories create the illusion of file drawers, even though the files may be physically dispersed.

Discussion Group A forum in which subscribers communicate by exchanging group E-mail messages.

Domain A portion of the hierarchical system used for identifying Internet addresses. Key domains include: .COM (commercial), .EDU (educational), .NET (network operations), .GOV (government), and .MIL (military).

Domain Name System (DNS) The system for translating alphabetic computer addresses into numerical addresses.

Download To receive information or files from a remote computer.

E-mail Electronic mail.

Electronic texts Texts encoded for electronic storage or transmission.

Emoticon A symbol used to indicate emotion or the equivalent of a voice inflection in an E-mail message. *See also* Smiley.

Encode To convert a file from one format to another, as from binary to ASCII for E-mail transmission.

Encryption The coding of data for purposes of secrecy and/or security.

Extension An abbreviation (usually three-digit) added to file names to indicate the file format.

FAQ *See* Frequently asked question.

File Stored computer data representing text, numeric, sound, or graphic images.

File transfer protocol (FTP) A program for transferring files from one computer (a host) to another (a client), especially for retrieving files from public archives. *See also* Anonymous FTP.

Frequently asked question (FAQ) A common name for files compiling answers to common questions, hence providing introductory information on a topic. Often appearing in newsgroups.

FTP *See* File transfer protocol.

Gateway A device, program, or site providing access to a network, generally between otherwise incompatible formats or protocols.

Gopher A hierarchical menu program for accessing information across the Internet.

Gopherspace That part of the Internet accessible by Gopher, that is, on Gopher servers and listed in Gopher menus.

Graphic interface A computer interface that displays graphic elements and icons rather than only lines of simple text. A computer interface negotiated with a mouse as well as with cursor keys.

Home page An initial menu page of a World Wide Web site, written in Hypertext Markup Language (HTML).

Host A computer that allows other computers to communicate with it.

Hypertext Markup Language (HTML) The system of embedding retrieval commands and associated addresses within a text; used for documents on the World Wide Web.

Hypertext Transfer Protocol (HTTP) The program controlling the transmission of documents and other files over the World Wide Web.

Hytelnet A menu-driven version of telnet. A menu of telnet sites.

Icon A graphical representation or symbol representing a file, program, or command on graphic-interface programs.

Interface The connection between two devices. More particularly, the nature of the display screen used for communication between user and computer.

Internet The worldwide "network of networks" connected to each other using the Internet protocol and other similar protocols. The Internet provides file transfer, remote login, electronic mail, and other services.

Internet Protocol (IP) A protocol involving packets of data traversing multiple networks. The protocol on which the Internet is based.

Internet Service Provider A national or local company providing access to the Internet.

Internet Society (ISOC) A nonprofit, professional membership organization that sets Internet policy and promotes its use through forums and the collaboration of members.

IP *See* Internet Protocol.

IP address The 32-bit address, defined by the Internet Protocol and represented in dotted decimal notation, cf.

171.292.292.23, assigned to a computer on a TCP/IP network.

Jughead (Jonzy's Universal Gopher Hierarchy Excavation and Display) A variant of Veronica that searches directories on a select number of Gophers.

Key-word search program A program for searching a database or set of files for a specific term or terms.

Listserv One of a number of listserver programs.

Listserver An automated mailing list distribution program providing the basis of many mailing list subscription or discussion groups.

Logoff To relinquish access to a computer network.

Logon To gain access to a remote computer or computer network.

Mailing list A system of forwarding messages to groups of people via E-mail.

Microsoft Windows A graphic-interface operating system from Microsoft Corporation for IBM-compatible computers.

Modem (Modulate/Demodulate) A device that enables computers to transmit and receive information over telephone lines by converting between digital and analog signals.

Mosaic The initial World Wide Web browser program.

Multimedia Integrating text, sound, and graphics.

Netiquette Proper social behavior on a network.

Netscape A leading World Wide Web browser program.

Network A communication system consisting of two or more computers or other devices.

Network Information Centers (NICs) Organizations providing documentation, guidance, advice, and assistance for a specific network.

Ntalk New talk, a new form of talk program. *See also* Talk.

On Ramp *See* Gateway.

On-line service A centralized computer network offering subscribers a variety of services including E-mail, file transfers, chat groups, and business, entertainment, and educational materials. Any service accessed by telephone.

Operating system The primary program of a computer, cf. MS-DOS, Windows, Macintosh System 7. The operating system determines the basic commands and the appearance of the screen.

Prompt A message or signal in a computer program requesting action by the user.

Protocol A formal description of operating rules.

Search program Any program providing direct examination of a database.

Server A host computer serving a special function or offering resources for client computers, whether as a storage device in a local area network or as a Gopher site on the Internet.

Shareware Commercial software available initially free on a trial basis.

Smiley An icon used to convey emotion or innuendo in texts, e.g., :-) (glad), :-[(disappointment).

Spamming Deluging someone with unwanted messages as punishment for inappropriate use of an on-line service or the Internet.

Surfing Random or otherwise seemingly undirected browsing, as of the World Wide Web.

Talk A program in which two users exchange on-screen messages.

Telnet An Internet program for accessing remote computers.

Text interface A screen display limited to lines of keyboard characters.

Uniform resource locator (URL) A format for indicating the protocol and address for accessing information on the Internet; a name identifying documents and services on the Internet.

Unix   A popular operating system important in the development of the Internet.

Upload   To send files to a remote computer.

URL   *See* Uniform resource locator.

Usenet   A network and program for reading and posting messages on public newsgroups; accessible in whole or in part via the Internet or many on-line services.

Veronica(Very Easy Rodent-Oriented Net-Wide Index of Computerized Archives)   A program developed at the University of Nevada at Reno in late 1992 for searching Gopher menus.

Wide Area Information Server (WAIS)   A program for searching collections of documents for specific terms.

Word processor   A computer program that replaces all the operations formerly associated with a typewriter.

World Wide Web (WWW)   A hypertext-based system for finding and accessing Internet resources.

SECTION TWO

Introduction

The following pages list Internet sites of interest to students in college success or freshman year experience courses. As with any listing of Internet resources, a number of cautions are in order.

The Internet sites listed here are almost exclusively on the World Wide Web. While the Web is the most graphic and visual service on the Internet, you may make equal use of e-mail, listserver mail discussion groups, or USENET newsgroup postings. (See the search programs listed below.)

While surfing these links, do not forget to investigate the resources available to you at you own institution. A school web page or gopher server might offer access to your college handbook and other documents, listings of campus organizations and/or events, resources from the placement office or health center, as well as online library information. The Internet may put you in contact with national support groups; your campus bulletin board may be able to put you in contact with local groups.

The Internet is not always the best or quickest source of information. Access to the Internet can never fully replace turning to the telephone yellow pages, visiting your college placement office, or using text search facilities on CD-ROM or proprietary on-line services (such as Lexis/Nexis) at your library.

Finally, remember that while the Internet is often an excellent source of information, of facts, data, statistics, and documents, it is not as useful for advice on how to live your life. That you must determine for yourself.

Note: If a site goes to two lines on the page in this book, do not key in an extra space between the two lines when entering the address on your computer.

Internet Sites

KNOW THYSELF: VALUES, GOALS, AND LEARNING STYLES

Academic Freedom

About Civil Liberty Index
http://www.eff.org/CAF/about.cli.html
Links to articles about civil liberties

Freedom of Speech and Academic Freedom
http://www.ucsc.edu/scomm/frsp.html
Links to a variety of sites on academic freedom and freedom of speech

Academic Freedom and Campus Speech Codes
http://www.uark.edu/depts/comminfo/www/academic.html
Links from the American Communication Association

Liberal Arts Education

Various Comments about Liberal Arts Education
http://www-hl.syr.edu/about/Libart.html

Why Study the Liberal Arts?
http://www2.environs.com:443/talbot/liberalarts1.html
Commentary by Leon Botstein, President of Bard College

Critical Thinking

Three Definitions of Critical Thinking
http://www.sonoma.edu/CThink/University/univlibrary/definect.nclk

The Center for Critical Thinking
http://www.sonoma.edu/cthink/university/univlibrary/library.nclk
Resources and discussion of the fundamentals of critical thinking from the Center for Critical Thinking at Sonoma State University

Goal Setting

Making the Transition to Higher Education: Setting and Achieving Goals
http://www.nus.sg/NUSinfo/CDTL/UFM/Orient/ Es2_1_3.html#ws2_1_3a
Suggestions for achieving goals and strategies for self-motivation

Goal Setting—Planning and Achieving Personal Ambitions
http://www.gasou.edu/psychweb/mtsite/page6.html
Links to articles on setting and achieving goals

Decision Making

Decision Theory and Decision Trees
http://www.gasou.edu/psychweb/mtsite/dectree.html

Critical Path Analysis
http://www.gasou.edu/psychweb/mtsite/critpath.html

Brainstorming
http://www.gasou.edu/psychweb/mtsite/brainstm.html

Strengths, Weaknesses, Opportunities, Threats (SWOT) Analysis
http://www.gasou.edu/psychweb/mtsite/swot.html

Learning Styles

Seven Styles of Learning
http://www.wordsimages.com/ewinters/styles.htm

Learning Style Inventory
http://www.hcc.hawaii.edu/hccinfo/facdev/lsi.html

Explanation of Learning Styles
http://www.sciences.drexel.edu/dcli/StudySkills/LearningStyles.html
Covers concrete experience, reflective observation, abstract conceptualization, and active experimentation, with examples

Learning Styles
http://hector.edfac.unimelb.edu.au/stats/questions/learningStyles.html
Covers activists (active experimentation), reflectors (reflective observation), theorists (abstract conceptualisation), pragmatists (concrete experience)

Major Categories in the Taxonomy of Educational Objectives
http://weber.u.washington.edu/~krumme/guides/bloom.html
Includes links to other sites discussing Bloom's classic taxonomy

Holland's Personality Life-Styles
http://www.bsu.edu/careers/holland.html

Gardner's Seven Types of Intelligence
http://klingon.util.utexas.edu/TAG/7_Intelligences.html

Learning Assumptions
http://www.hcc.hawaii.edu/hccinfo/facdev/LearnAssump.html
Assumptions fundamental to planning an education program

Thirty Things We Know for Sure about Adult Learners
http://www.hcc.hawaii.edu/hccinfo/facdev/30things.html

Personality Assessment

MetaSelf–A Visual Aid to Being Human
http://www.dnai.com/model/
A visual model of the self and its place in the world

Personality Type Summary
http://www.pendulum.org/misc/mb.htm#V
Descriptions of four scales for personality typing

Myers-Briggs Type Indicator
http://www.ccens.com/mbti.htm
Discussion of the Myers-Briggs Index

Myers-Briggs Type Index Calculator
http://www.hotfiles.com/swbrowse/000/A/B/swlib-000ABI.html
A program requiring Windows 95 software

Kiersey Temperament Sorter
http://longwood.cs.ucf.edu/~porthous/mb_test.shtml*
An online version with 70 questions and scoring

On Learning Styles
http://www.gsu.edu/~dschjb/wwwmbti.html
The four dimensions underlying the Myers-Briggs Type Indicator (MBTI), and teaching approaches applicable for different MBTI profiles

TIME MANAGEMENT

Checklists and Guides

Time Management Checklist
http://www.csbsju.edu/advising/help/tm-check.html

Time Management Skills
http://www.gasou.edu/psychweb/mtsite/page5.html
"How to Get the Most Out of Your Time" and "Specific Time Management Tools"

Twenty-Three Time Management Techniques
http://www.csbsju.edu/advising/help/23tmt.html

Ten Tips for Improving Time Management
http://www.dartmouth.edu/admin/acskills/time_tips.html

Procrastination

Techniques To Manage Procrastination
http://128.32.89.153/CalREN/procrastechniques.html

Procrastination Research Group
http://superior.carleton.ca/~tpychyl/
Information and research related to procrastination, from Carleton University, Ottawa, Canada

Procrastinator's Creed
http://www.eskimo.com/~spban/creed.html
Humorous

LEARNING THE COLLEGE SYSTEM

Starting Out

Articles on Starting College
http://www2.environs.com:443/talbot/toart.html

The On-line Student Survival Guide
http://www.luminet.net/~jackp/survive.html
"An Internet Resource Guide for Success in College"

Strategies for Success
http://www.reg.uci.edu/UCI/HONORS/CHP_HANDBOOK/success.html

Going to College Is Easier Than It Looks
http://pegasus.cc.ucf.edu/~rla/fillers/collegeismorethan.htm
Commentary by Ashley Wilson, Carnegie Mellon University

Student Codes of Conduct
http://www.smu.edu/~stulife/studentcode.html
From Southern Methodist University, covering everything from
drugs to noise and bicycle policies

Peterson's Annual Survey of Undergraduate Institutions
http://www.petersons.com/resources/ugedu.html#enrollment
Statistical data on enrollment, faculty, fees, etc.

College-Level Entrance Exam (CLEP)

What Is CLEP?
http://www.collegeboard.org/clep/html/indx001.html
A description of the exam, test centers, and list of colleges granting
credit

Guides

How To Succeed as a Student
http://www.gu.edu.au/gwis/stubod/stuadv/stu_advice_con.html
Discussion of the university and classroom structure, the role of the
student, first year subjects, how to study and learn, preparing and
presenting assignments, and some tools of the trade. Originally written for students at Griffith University, Australia

The National Clearinghouse for Academic Advising
http://www.uvc.ohio-state.edu/Chouse.html
Annotated bibliographies covering academic advising topics

The Source
http://www.unc.edu/student/source/
From the University of North Carolina, Chapel Hill

Freshman Year Academic Advising Manual
http://www.salc.wsu.edu/advising/academicam/index.html
From the Student Advising and Learning Center, Washington State
University

Student-Teacher Relationships

Choosing Professors
http://weber.u.washington.edu/~uwired/classes/msaedi/Profesors.html
From the University of Washington Freshman Survival Guide

How To Identify and Cultivate a Faculty Mentor
http://www.reg.uci.edu/UCI/HONORS/CHP_HANDBOOK/
fac_mentor.html

Tips On Dealing with Faculty, In The Classroom And Outside
http://www.reg.uci.edu/UCI/HONORS/CHP_HANDBOOK/
tips_on_fac.html

Choosing a Major

Exploring Majors
http://www.gmu.edu/student/asst/expmajors.html
From George Mason University–a large file (216K)

Choosing and Using Your Major
gopher://minerva.acc.virgina.edu/00/pubs/career/handouts/1/6

The Major Resource Kit
gopher://gopher.udel.edu/11/.dept/carserv/MRkit
From the University of Delaware

How To Choose a Major
http://www.salc.wsu.edu/advising/academicam/info/htcam.html

Choosing a College Major
http://weber.u.washington.edu/~uwired/classes/triordan/triordan.html
From the University of Washington Freshman Survival Guide

STUDY SKILLS

Study Skills Checklists

Study Skill Checklist
http://www.ucc.vt.edu/stdysk/checklis.html
Test-taking and problem-solving tips

Study Skills Survey
http://www.d.umn.edu/student/loon/acad/strat/self_test.html

College Study Skills Guides

University of California, Berkeley, Student Learning Center
http://128.32.89.153/CalRENHP.html
Tips and exercises to help develop better study strategies and habits

**College of Saint Benedict and Saint John's University
Study Skills Guides**
http://www.csbsju.edu/advising/helplist.html

Dartmouth Study Skills Guide Menu
http://www.dartmouth.edu/admin/acskills/index.html#study

University of Texas, Austin, Learning Skills Center Study Tips
http://www.utexas.edu/student/lsc/handouts/stutips.html

**Virginia Polytechnic Institute Study Skills
Self-Help Information**
http://www.ucc.vt.edu/stdysk/stdyhlp.html

University of Minnesota, Duluth, Study Strategies Homepage
http://www.d.umn.edu/student/loon/acad/strat/study_strat_enr.html

Listening Skills and Notetaking

Effective Listening
http://www.csbsju.edu/advising/help/eff-list.html
11 basic principles and the five R'S of notetaking

Cornell Notetaking System
http://www.dartmouth.edu/admin/acskills/cornell.html
The 5 R's of note-taking

Lecture Note Taking
http://www.csbsju.edu/advising/help/lec-note.html

Underlinging/Highlighting
http://www.csbsju.edu/advising/help/underlin.html

Note-Taking and In-Class Skills
http://www.ucc.vt.edu/stdysk/notetake.html

Note-Taking Stategies
http://ecuvax.cis.ecu.edu/academics/schdept/unstud/asc/notetake.htm

Memory

Ten Principles of Memory
http://www.dartmouth.edu/admin/acskills/memory.html

Memory Theory and Techniques
http://www.gasou.edu/psychweb/mtsite/memory.html
Numerous links to articles on memory techniques and their applications

Eight Strategy Families
*http://www.4j.lane.edu/RTT/OnLineInservice/ed2000/
StrategyFamilies.html*
Including focusing, remembering, analyzing, and evaluating strategies

Studying

Study Distractions Analysis
http://www.vt.edu:10021/studentinfo/ucc/studydis.html

Some Ways to Get More Out of Studying
http://www.csbsju.edu/advising/help/getmore.html

Study Formula SQ3R
http://www.csbsju.edu/advising/help/sq3r.html

Test Taking

How To Keep Calm During Tests
http://www.utexas.edu/student/lsc/handouts/1305.html

Test Taking Skills: Effective Study Techniques for Essay Tests
http://www.csbsju.edu/advising/help/testskil.html

Test-Taking Strategies
http://www.csbsju.edu/advising/help/teststrt.html

Test Taking Strategies
http://ecuvax.cis.ecu.edu/academics/schdept/unstud/asc/testtake.htm

READING AND WRITING

Reading Techniques

Six Reading Myths
http://www.dartmouth.edu/admin/acskills/reading.html

Skimming
http://www.csbsju.edu/advising/help/skimming.html

P-R-R (Preview-Read-Recall)
http://www.utexas.edu/student/lsc/handouts/1422.html
"How to Read Your Textbook More Efficiently"

Thoughts on Speed Reading
http://www.utexas.edu/student/lsc/handouts/529.html

Writing

How to Write and Revise a Rough Draft
http://www.utexas.edu/student/lsc/handouts/1234.html

Writers' Resources On The Web
http://www.interlog.com/~ohi/www/writesource.html
Categorized by subject

Grammar and Style Notes
http://www.english.upenn.edu/~jlynch/grammar.html
An extensive miscellany of grammatical rules and explanations,
comments on style, and suggestions on usage

University of Michigan's Online Writing Lab Resources
http://www-personal.umich.edu/~nesta/OWL/Resources.html

Harvard Writing Center Writing Tools
http://www.fas.harvard.edu/~wricntr/wtools.html

The Elements of Style.
http://www.cc.columbia.edu/acis/bartleby/strunk/
William Strunk Jr.'s classic (1918 edition)

Online Writing Labs (OWLs)

Purdue University's OWL
http://owl.trc.purdue.edu/
Including Indexes for Writers, Online Reference Resources, Guides
to Style and Editing, Business & Technical Writing, Professional
Organizations, ESL-Related Sites, and Listserv Groups

University of Texas, Austin, Undergraduate Writing Center
http://www.utexas.edu/depts/uwc/.html/main.html
Guides and handouts

University of Florida Writing Environment
http://www.ucet.ufl.edu:80/writing/nwe.html

University of Maine Writing Center Online
http://www.ume.maine.edu/~wcenter/

On-Line Dictionairies

Merriam Webster Online
http://www.m-w.com

Index of On-Line Dictionaries
http://www.bucknell.edu/~rbeard/diction.html
An index of on-line dictionaries,thesauri, and other reference works
for a wide variety of languages

Plagiarism

Avoiding Plagiarism
http://www.hamilton.edu/html/academic/resource/wc/
AvoidingPlagiarism.html
With examples

Plagiarism and Collusion
http://134.115.16.1/~winzar/Teaching/collude.htm

Avoiding Plagiarism: Using Sources Properly
http://harpo.tnstate.edu/~jordan/sources.html

An Introduction to Copyright Issues for World Wide Web publishers
http://riceinfo.rice.edu/about/copyright.html

Plagiarism
http://cwis.lawrence.edu/www/campus/sas/plag.html

Plagiarism and the Web
http://http.ecn.bgu.edu/users/mfbhl/wiu/plagiarism.htm
Discussion of repositories for plagiarisable papers and what teachers can do about them

Citing Internet Sources

MLA Guidelines for Citation from the Internet
http://www.cas.usf.edu/english/walker/mla.html

Guide to Citing Internet Sources
http://www.bournemouth.ac.uk/service-depts/lis/LIS_Pub/harvardsystint.html

Guide for Citing Electronic Information
http://www.wilpaterson.edu/wpcpages/library/citing.htm

PROBLEM SOLVING AND MATHEMATICS

Mathematics

On-Line Mathematics Resources
http://euclid.math.fsu.edu/Science/General.html

Math Meta-Index
http://euclid.math.fsu.edu/Science/math.html
Meta-Index to mathematics resources on the Internet

Catalog of Mathematics Resources on WWW and the Internet
http://mthwww.uwc.edu/wwwmahes/files/math01.htm

Understanding Mathematics
http://www.math.utah.edu/~alfeld/math.html
A major study guide, by Peter Alfeld, University of Utah

Success in Mathematics
http://euler.slu.edu/Dept/SuccessinMath.html#taketest
Tips on how to study mathematics, how to approach problem-solving, and how to study for and take tests

The Geometry Center Gallery of Interactive Geometry
http://www.geom.umn.edu/
Ten web-based applications that explore different aspects of geometry

Statistics Every Writer Should Know
http://nilesonline.com/stats/

Frank Potter's Science Gems
http://www-sci.lib.uci.edu/SEP/SEP.html
Links to 2,000 science/mathematics-related resources

Problem Solving

How to Solve It
http://www.math.utah.edu/~alfeld/math/polya.html
A summary of Polya's classic text describing a four-stage approach to mathematical problem-solving based on common-sense questions

Los Alamos National Laboratory Mega-Mathematics
http://www.c3.lanl.gov/mega-math/
Resources on problem-solving, graphing, logic, etc.

COMPUTING FOR COLLEGE SUCCESS: TECHNOLOGY ON CAMPUS

General

Use a Computer? Me?
http://www.rtt.ab.ca/rtt/sjtown/final/tech.html
Links to instructions for getting started on the Internet

Internet Hoaxes
http://ciac.llnl.gov/ciac/bulletins/h-05.shtml

Computer Virus Myths Page
http://www.kumite.com/myths/

Accessing the Internet by E-Mail
http://www.magicnet.net/~fortna/email_1.html
Dr. Bob's Guide to Offline Internet Access, for users without full Internet access

Library Catalogs

Accesses to Major English-Language Libraries On-Line
http://www.clark.net/pub/abaa-booknet/research/librar.html

Library Research Guides
http://frank.mtsu.edu/~kmiddlet/libweb/libresgd.html
Including links to both local library and Internet resources

Library and Information Science Resources
http://lcweb.loc.gov/global/library/

Online Catalogs with 'Webbed' Interfaces
http://www.lib.ncsu.edu/staff/morgan/alcuin/wwwed-catalogs.html
Intended primarily as a resource for librarians

Internet Etiquette (Netiquette)

The Net: User Guidelines and Netiquette
http://rs6000.adm.fau.edu/rinaldi/net/index.htm
E-mail, listserver mailing list, and newgroup search programs

How to Find Someone's E-mail Address
http://dantzig.ee.ucla.edu/misc/eaddress.html

Internet E-Mail Resource Page
http://www.ronin.com/pa-software/

Introduction to Mailing Lists
http://www.gold.ac.uk/guides/c701.html

The Liszt
http://www.liszt.com/search
Search program for over 54,000 electronic mail discussion groups

DejaNews
http://www.dejanews.com/forms/dnquery.html
Search program for postings to all USENET newsgroups

Searching the World Wide Web

The Most Comprehensive Search Center on the Internet
http://www.nedsite.nl/search/search.htm
Links to search programs for all aspects of the Internet

Internet Navigation
http://riceinfo.rice.edu/Internet/
Rice University guide to search tools for the Internet, with recommendations

Info, Where Are You?
http://www.zdnet.com/pccomp/features/internet/search/sub2.html
Choosing the best search engine for your needs

The Spiders's Apprentice–How to Use Web Search Engines
http://www.monash.com/spidap4.html

Internet Search Tools Details
http://sunsite.berkeley.edu/Help/searchdetails.html

Evaluation of Selected Internet Search Tools
http://www.library.nwu.edu/resources/internet/search/evaluate.html

Understanding and Comparing Web Search Tools
http://www.hamline.edu/library/bush/handouts/comparisons.html
A bibliography of journal articles, with links

Annotated List of Web Search Tools
http://www.jobweb.org/catapult/search.htm
With links to each

Advanced Web Searching: Tricks of the Trade
http://www.onlineinc.com/onlinemag/MayOL/zorn5.html
Includes charts and examples

Miscellaneous Search Tools

Clearinghouse for Subject-Oriented Internet Resource Guides
http://www.clearinghouse.net

Electronic Reference Desk
http://infoshare1.princeton.edu:2003/vlib/erefdesk/Eref3.html
Princeton University collection of on-line reference works

How Much, How Many? Statistical Sources and Calculation Tools on the Net
http://www.sau.edu/cwis/internet/wild/Refdesk/Stats/staindex.htm

Biographical Sources
http://www.sau.edu/cwis/internet/wild/Refdesk/Biograph/bioindex.htm

FedWorld
http://www.fedworld.gov/
All-encompassing Federal Government home page

Government Information Locator (GILS)
http://info.er.usgs.gov/public/gils/intro.html
Identifies and describes information resources throughout the Federal government

World Wide Web Literacy

Checklist for an Informational Web Page
http://www.science.widener.edu/~withers/inform.htm
Questions to ask about the usefullness and objectivity of a web page

Checklist for a News Web Page
http://www.science.widener.edu/~withers/news.htm
How to evaluate the authority, coverage, objectivity, and accuracy of news pages

Evaluating Web Pages: Links to Examples of Various Concepts
http://www.science.widener.edu/~withers/examples.htm

PLANNING YOUR CAREER

Major Career Guides

The Definitive Guide to Internet Career Resources
http://phoenix.placement.oakland.edu/career/internet.htm#c

JobWeb
http://www.jobweb.org/catapult/catapult.htm

The Riley Guide to Employment Opportunities and Job Resources on the Internet
http://www.jobtrak.com/jobguide/

Bureau of Labor Statistics 1996-97 Occupational Outlook Handbook
http://stats.bls.gov:80/ocohome.htm

Career Assessment

ACT Interest Inventory and Student Profile
http://www.d.umn.edu/student/loon/car/self/career_act_ii.html
ACT test scores are linked to occupations and programs of study

Merkler Career Interest Inventory
http://icpac.indiana.edu/htdocs/careers/merkler.html

Discovering Careers That Fit You
http://icpac.indiana.edu/htdocs/infoseries/is-50.html
Holland Code interest inventory exercise and scoring

Transferable Skills Survey
http://www.d.umn.edu/student/loon/car/self/career_transfer_survey.html

Career Resource Centers

Career Resource Center
http://www.careers.org/crc_new.html

University of California at Berkeley Career Exploration Links
http://www.uhs.berkeley.edu/CareerLibrary/links/careerme.htm

University of Manitoba Carrer Resources Center
http://www.umanitoba.ca/student/counselling/crc.html

Boise State University Career Center
http://www.idbsu.edu/career/wwwcctr.html

Career Magazine index and links
http://www.careermag.com:80/links.html

Career Profiles

Index of Occupations by Name
http://www.etc.bc.ca/provdocs/jobfutures/TitleIndex.html
Listing of hundreds of occupational categories

Exploring Occupations: Getting You Started on Your Career Path!
http://www.umanitoba.ca/counselling/careers.html

Indiana Career and Postsecondary Advancement Center ICPAC) Career Profiles
http://icpac.indiana.edu/htdocs/careers/cs_series.html

Professional Occupational Outlook Handbook of Descriptions and Job Outlooks
http://www.espan.com/docs/doot1.html

Career and Educationsal Guidance Library, Career Exploration Links
http://www.uhs.berkeley.edu/CareerLibrary/links/careerme.htm

Resume Writing

Career Resource Center Resume Writing Center Guides
http://www.careermosaic.com/cm/crc/crc15.html

Resume Proofreading Checklist
http://www.careermosaic.com/cm/cc/cc19.html

Job Hunting

The Job Search Process
http://www.jobtrak.com/jobsearch_docs/pointers.html
An extensive guide to all phases of job searching

Links to Tools for Job Hunting
http://www.interbiznet.com/hunt/tools.html

Career Fairs Clearninghouse
http://www.jobweb.org/cfairsr.htm
A database searchable by state or month

CareerCity's Search Engine
http://www.adamsonline.com/
Job listings by profession and state

Business Sites on the Web
http://www.jobweb.org/catapult/emplyer.htm

Internships

Lifelong Learning Internships
http://www.tripod.com/work/internships/
A database searchable by interest and location

Getting Your Feet Wet: How Internships Give You Experience
http://www.futurescan.com/index.html

Internship Opportunities
HREF="http://www.contact.org/IS/intern_search.html
Search program for internship opportunities

Summer Jobs

Summer Jobs, Internships, Fieldwork & Postgraduate Options
http://www.jobweb.org/catapult/jintern.htm

Summer Jobs
http://www.summerjobs.com/
A searchable database of seasonal and part-time job opportunities

Overseas Jobs

Overseas Jobs Express
http://www.overseasjobs.com/
Over 700 links to employment resources in over 40 countries

ACHIEVING RELATIONSHIPS IN A MULTI-CULTURAL WORLD: DIVERSITY ON CAMPUS

Statistics

Postsecondary Education 1995 Digest of Education Statistics
http://www.ed.gov/NCES/pubs/D95/dintro3.html
Statistics on all aspects of postsecondary education

Annual High School Dropout Rates by Sex, Race, Grade, and Hispanic Origin: October 1967 to 1994
http://www.census.gov/population/socdemo/school/tablea-4.txt

Persons 14 to 24 Years Old by High School Graduate Status, College Enrollment, Attainment, Sex, Race, and Hispanic Origin
http://www.census.gov/population/socdemo/school/tablea-5.txt

The Nation: Demographics
http://chronicle.merit.edu/.almanac/.almdem2.html
Breakdown by age groups, racial and ethnic identity, and education level

The Nation: Students
http://chronicle.merit.edu/.almanac/.almstu5.html
Breakdown by ethincity and type of institution

Facts and Figures on U.S. Higher Education
http://galen.library.ucsf.edu/kr/subs/stat/ushighered.html
A statistical portrait of U.S. colleges and universities

Diversity Resources

Education and Cultural Diversity
http://iscssun.uni.edu/teachctr/diversit.html
A short history and bibliography

Multicultural Resources
http://www.public.iastate.edu/~savega/multicul.htm
Links to a wide variety of multicultural sites and resources

Multicultural Education: Selected Sources for Research
http://lweb.tc.columbia.edu/reference/guides/multi/
Extensive links from Teachers College, Columbia University

Diversity Resources
http://latino.sscnet.ucla.edu/diversity1.html
Links to a broad range of Internet resources

Multicultural Sites
http://www.cnet.com/Content/Features/Net/Rainbow/ss6.html

Gender & Race in Media: Assorted Gender & Media links
http://www3.arcade.uiowa.edu/gw/comm/GenderMedia/assorted.html

Gender & Race in Media:Television & Film
http://www3.arcade.uiowa.edu/gw/comm/GenderMedia/tvfilm.html

The American-Arab Anti-Discrimination Committee
http://205.177.10.11/adc/

Webcrawler "Life and Leisure–Religion" Links
http://www.webcrawler.com/select/life.relig.html

Antisemitism links
http://ucsu.colorado.edu/~jsu/antisemitism.html

Answers to Your Questions About Sexual Orientation and Homosexuality
http://www.pe.net/~bidstrup/psych.htm
From the American Psychological Association

The Cool Page For Queer Teens!
http://www.pe.net/~bidstrup/cooldat.htm
Answers to questions, and resources

Specific Groups

Universal Black Pages
http://www.gatech.edu/bgsa/blackpages.html

Asian-American Resources
http://www.mit.edu:8001/afs/athena.mit.edu/user/i/r/irie/www/aar.html

Hispanic Resources Center
http://www.hooked.net/saludos/LINKS.html

LatinoLink
http://www.latinolink.com/

The Greek Pages
http://www.greekpages.com/
Information and links on fraternities

Resources for the Disabled
http://www.aip.org/aip/urls/disable.html

PlanetOut
http://www.planetout.com
Offering gays comfort, support, community, and identity

Ultimate Jewish/Israel Link Launcher
http://ucsu.colorado.edu/~jsu/launcher.html

Women Department
http://www.ypn.com/women
Comprehensive guide to Web sites, newsgroups, and mailing lists

The Rhythmn of the Net
http://www.ypn.com/topics/7641.html
Extensive women's links

Relationships

Marriage & Relationships Related Links
http://www.whidbey.net/southern/family.htm
Resources on marriage and relationships

Family Relations
http://www.personal.psu.edu/faculty/n/x/nxd10/family3.htm
Including links on marriage and dating, parenting, and family problems like alcoholism, child abuse, and family violence

Adolescence Directory On-Line (ADOL)
http://education.indiana.edu/cas/adol/adol.html
Guide to information on adolescent issues, from the Center for Adolescent Studies, Indiana University

Campus Activities

Internet Headquarters for Student Governments
http://www.umr.edu/stugov.html
Connecting and supporting student governments

Campus Outreach Opportunity League
http://www.cool2serve.org/
A national non-profit organization that helps college students start, strengthen, and expand community service programs

ASSURING YOUR PHYSICAL HEALTH

Diet / Nutrition

Eating Well: What to Eat and When to Eat It
http://www.worldguide.com/Fitness/nut.htmlbasicx
Nutritional guidelines

Duke University Nutrition
http://h-devil-www.mc.duke.edu/h-devil/nutrit/nutrit.htm
Various topics related to nutritional health

CyberNutrition Online
http://chd.syr.edu/chd/CyberNutrition2.html
Answers to questions related to food, nutrition, and diet, provided by
Syracuse University College for Human Development Nutrition and
Foodservice Management Department students

The Something-Fishy Website on Eating Disorders
http://www.something-fishy.com/ed.htm
Discussion of all eating disorders, with extensive links to additional
resources

Major Sources

**Duke University "Healthy Devil"On-Line Guide
to Health Concerns**
http://h-devil-www.mc.duke.edu/h-devil/

Fronske Health Center, Northern Arizona University
http://www.nau.edu/~fronske/

**New York Online Access to Health (NOAH) Health Topics
General Index**
http://www.noah.cuny.edu/qksearch.html
In English and Spanish

"The Best Medical Resources on the Web"
http://www.cityscape.co.uk/journals/other.htm

Yahoo Health search categories
http://www.yahoo.com/health/

HealthNews
http://www.healthnet.ivi.com/ivi/hnews/common/htm/index.htm
A major health news resource from the publishers of the New England Journal of Medicine

Mayo Health Oasis Library of Resources
http://www.mayo.ivi.com/ivi/mayo/common/htm/library.htm

WellnessWeb
http://www.wellweb.com/preview/zpre.htm
A collaboration of patients, healthcare professionals, and other
caregivers

The Alternative Medicine Home Page
http://www.pitt.edu/~cbw/altm.html
Links to alternative medicine resources.

First Aid
http://www.prairienet.org/~cicely/firstaid/

Prevention

Prevention Primer
http://www.health.org/pubs/PRIMER/toc.htm

Wisconsin Clearinghouse for Prevention Resources
http://www.uhs.wisc.edu/wch/
Educational materials from the University Health Services,
University of Wisconsin, Madison

National Health Organizations

U. S. Health Resources
http://www.contact.org/ushealth.htm
Links to national health organizations and associations, guides,
and directories

National Hotlines and Service Organizations
http://www.thebody.com/hotlines/national.html

Women's Health Issues

HealthWise Forum for Women's Health
http://www.healthwire.com/women/
A collection of facts, information, advice, and suggestions to help
women deal with health concerns

Guide To Women's Health Issues
http://www.lib.umich.edu/chdocs/womenhealth/old/
womens_health.html
Covering emotional, physical, and sexual issues

WWWomen
http://www.wwwomen.com/
"The Premier Search Directory for Women Online"

Women's Health
http://h-devil-www.mc.duke.edu/h-devil/women/women.htm
Topics from the Duke University Healthy Devil Online

Maternal and Child Health Network
gopher://mchnet.ichp.ufl.edu

ASSURING YOUR MENTAL HEALTH

General Resources

Self-Help Home Page
http://wings.buffalo.edu/student-life/ccenter/http://ub-counseling.buffalo.edu/
From the State University of New York at Buffalo Counseling Center

MentalHealth.com
http://www.mentalhealth.com/p1.html
An encyclopedia of mental health information

Mental Health Center Index of Self-Help Resources/Links
http://www.cmhc.com/selfhelp.htm
A very extensive list of links to organizations and people offering local support groups

Psychology Self-Help Resources on the Internet
http://www.gasou.edu/psychweb/resource/selfhelp.htm
Links to non-commercial sites providing information and help about specific disorders related to psychology

Psych Central: Dr. Grohol's Mental Health Page
http://www.coil.com/~grohol/
A major index for psychology, support, and mental health issues, resources, and people on the Internet

Mental Health Links on the Internet
http://www.unf.edu/dept/counseling_center/cool.html

Suicide Fact Sheet
http://www.intergate.com/~hotline/info.html#suicide

Homesickness

Ten Ways to Combat Homesickness on a College Campus
http://www.nau.edu/~fronske/homesick.html

Stress

Stress Fact Sheet
http://www.dartmouth.edu/admin/acskills/stress.html

Strategies for Stess Management
http://www.csbsju.edu/advising/help/stresmgt.html

Noodle's Panic-Anxiety Page
http://www.algy.com/anxiety/relax.html
Links to sites on coping, meditation, Yoga, nutrition, and general anxiety

Basic Guidelines for Coping with Stress and Anxiety
http://www.net-dot-com.com/midwest/stress.htm

SEXUAL CHOICES AND DECISIONS

AIDS

HIV & AIDS: The Basics
http://www.noah.cuny.edu/aids/gmhc/brochure7.html

The Biweekly AIDS Information Newsletter
http://www.cmpharm.ucsf.edu/%7Etroyer/safesex/vanews/
Distributed by the U.S. Department of Veterans Affairs, AIDS Information Center, at the San Francisco VA Medical Center

AIDS Education and General Information System (AEGIS)
gopher://gopher.hivnet.org

A Multimedia AIDS and HIV Information Source
http://www.thebody.com/cgi-bin/body.cgi
Links to discussion of all aspects of AIDS, its treatment, and quality of life issues

Condoms

Condom Country Catalog—How to Use a Condom
http://www.condom.com/Condom/Country/how_to_use|homepage| 12345678901234567891 13438145/
From the FDA Consumer Magazine

"The Condom Fact Sheet," "A Condom Could Save Your Life," and "Surgeon General's Report on AIDS"
http://www.condom.com/Condom/Country/government|homepage/
Government information provided by Condom Country

HIV, AIDS and Condoms
http://birmingham.gov.uk/html/helpline/health/hiv.html

Reproduction /Contraception

Planned Parenthood Federation of America
http://www.ppfa.org/ppfa/
Homepage of the world's oldest and largest voluntary family planning organization

National Abortion and Reproductive Rights Action League (NARAL)
http://www.naral.org/
Homepage with links to fact sheets

Duke University Pregnancy
http://h-devil-www.mc.duke.edu/h-devil/preg/preg.htm
Pregnancy testing, options, and suggested resources from Duke University "Healthy Devil" Online

Sexuality

Sex: Communication
http://h-devil-www.mc.duke.edu/h-devil/sex/sex.htm
Includes "Talking About Sex," "Abstinence–Are You Ready For Sex?," "Gay, Lesbian, And Bisexual Orientation," "Sexual Dysfunction," and "101 Ways To Please Your Lover Without 'Doing It,'" from the Duke University "Healthy Devil" Online

Sexuality Bytes
http://www.sexualitybytes.com.au/websex/adult/default.htm
An on-line encyclopedia of sex and sexual health

"Sexuality in a Culture of Confusion"
http://www.intac.com/~jdeck/habib
On-line photojournalism exhibit documenting youth culture and teen-age attitudes toward sexuality

Dr. Ruth's Sexnet
http://www.drruth.com/

Sexually Transmitted Diseases

Sexually Transmitted Disease (STD) Homepage
http://med-www.bu.edu/people/sycamore/std/
Links for AIDS, chancroid, chlamydia, gonorrhea, hepatitis b, herpes simplex, pubic lice and scabies, syphilis, trichomona, and venereal warts

The Safer Sex Pages
http://www.safersex.org/
Links to a variety of topics

STD links
http://h-devil-www.mc.duke.edu/h-devil/stds/stds.htm
From Duke University Healthy Devil Online

Chlamydia
http://server.berkeley.edu/Health/Illness/chlamyd.html
Symptoms, diagnosis, treatment, and prevention for the most common STD in the U.S. today

The Syphilis Information Page
http://students.missouri.edu/~shape/specinfs/syphilis.html

Sexual Assault and Harrassment

Sexual Harrassment–Myth and Reality
http://www.apa.org/pubinfo/harass.html
Guidelines on legal defintions, types, effects, and responses, from The American Psychological Association (APA)

Sexual Harassment links
http://tyco.cs.utk.edu/%7Ebartley/index/sexualHarassment/

"Friends" Raping Friends–Could It Happen to You?
http://www.cs.utk.edu/~bartley/acquaint/acquaintRape.html
All aspects of date rape–what it is, how it happens, how it can be avoided, and how to respond to it

The Cornell Women's Handbook: Protecting Ourselves
http://www.cio.cornell.edu:8000/cwh/ProtectingOurselves-f.html
Guidelines on rape, sexual assault, and other abusive relationships

Sexual Assault Information Page
http://www.cs.utk.edu/~bartley/saInfoPage.html
Covering acquaintance rape, child sexual abuse/assault, incest, rape, ritual abuse, sexual assault, and sexual harassment

Rape Crisis Center on the Web
http://tyco.cs.utk.edu/%7Ebartley/index/sexualAssault/crisisCenters/online/
With links by state

The National Coalition Against Sexual Assault (NCASA)
http://tyco.cs.utk.edu/%7Ebartley/ncasa/ncasa.html

Sexual Assault and Rape Crisis Resource List
http://www.feminist.org/911/sexass.html
By state

Rape, Sexual Assault, and Harassment
http://www.umn.edu/mincava/sah.htm
From the Minnesota Higher Education Center Against Violence and Abuse (MINCAVA)

Male Rape
http://www.ocs.mq.edu.au:80/~korman/feminism/malerape.html
An index of resources

Dating Violence and Acquaintance Assault
http://iunrwww.unl.edu/ianr/PUBS/nehfacts/nf244.htm
What it is and what you can do about it

Rape: Prevention & Resources
http://www.nau.edu/~fronske/rape.html
From the Fronske Health Center, Northern Arizona University

ALCOHOL, TOBACCO, DRUGS, AND CAMPUS SAFETY

Major Sources

Web of Addiction Fact Sheets
http://www.well.com/user/woa/facts.htm
Fact sheets index

The National Clearinghouse for Alcohol and Drug Information (NCADI)
http://www.health.org/
Alcohol, tobacco and other drug information materials provided
by the Center for Substance Abuse Prevention(CSAP), the world's
largest resource for current information and materials concerning
substance abuse prevention

METNET Drug Information Database
http://www.inform.umd.edu:8080/EdRes/Colleges/BSOS/
Depts/Cesar/metnet/general.htm
General information on addiction from the Center for Substance
Abuse Research (CESAR), Governor's Drug and Alcohol Abuse Com-
mission, University of Maryland.

Drinking

Self-Scoring Alcohol Checkup
http://www.cts.com/~habtsmrt/chkup.html

Warning Signs of Problem Drinking
http://www.columbia.edu/cu/healthwise/0338.html

Coping with the Killer Habits: Excessive Drinking and Alcoholism
http://www.medsource.com/con3.html
Discussion of excessive drinking, with links to Alcoholics Anonymous

Drinking and Smoking
http://h-devil-www.mc.duke.edu/h-devil/drugs/drugs.htm
From the Duke University "Healthy Devil" Online

Mothers Against Drunk Driving
http://www.gran-net.com/madd/madd.htm

Substance Abuse

Narcotics and Substance Abuse
http://www.usia.gov/topical/global/drugs/subab.htm
From the United States Information Service (USIS) Gateway to Information on Substance Abuse

Sedative–Hypnotics
http://www.well.com/user/woa/fsseda.htm
Fact sheet from the Missouri Department of Mental Health Division of Alcohol and Drug Abuse

Fact Sheet Rohypno
http://www.health.org/pubs/factsht/rohypnol.htm
From the National Institute on Drug Abuse

Women and Substance Abuse
http://www.well.com/user/woa/fswomen.htm
Fact sheet with links

Support Groups

Alcoholics Anonymous
http://www.alcoholics-anonymous.org/
Official Home page

Marijuana Anonymous
http://www.marijuana-anonymous.org
Official Home Page

Cocaine Anonymous
http://www.ca.org/
Official Home Page

Tobacco

QuitNet
http://www.quitnet.org/quitnetta/
Information, interactive tools, and support mechanisms to people
seeking to stop tobacco use

Tobacco Information.
http://charlotte.med.nyu.edu/woodr/tobacco.html
A collection of pages, including Brown & Willamson Tobacco
Corporation documents leaked to the University of California, San
Francisco

Assault (Non-Sexual)

Academic Crime Statistics Link Guide
http://www.crime.org/links_academic.html
Police crime statistics by college

Assault Prevention Information Network
http://galaxy.einet.net/galaxy/Community/Safety/Assault-Prevention/
apin/APINindex.html
With links to self-defense and martial arts sites

Thinking About Self-Defense
http://galaxy.einet.net/galaxy/Community/Safety/Assault-Prevention/
apin/NCASAGuidelines.html
National Coalition Against Sexual Assault (NCASA) guidelines for
choosing a self-defense course

The Best Defense Against Assault
http://www.nau.edu/~fronske/defense.html
Fronske Health Center handout

MANAGING MONEY

General

Are You In a 'Credit Crisis'?
http://www.nccs.org/quiz.html
A quiz to recognize the signs–and how to solve the problem

Topics on Keeping Your Finances in Check
http://www.taponline.com/tap/life/schools/features/ultimate/
chapter4-2.html

FTC Consumer Brochures
http://www.webcom.com/~lewrose/brochures.html

Credit Cards

FTC Consumer Brochures: Credit Fraud
http://192.216.46.51/select/persfin.22.html
Credit and credit card information pamphlets from the Federal
Trade Commission Office of Consumer and Business Education

Credit Card Info Index
http://www.amdream.com/credit/cardsetc.htm

A World Wide Web Resource For College Students
http://www.americanexpress.com/student
American Express student page

College Financing—General

FAQ: Financial Aid, Scholarships, and Fellowships
http://www.finaid.org/finaid/faqs/finaid.faq
Monthly posting of the Frequently Asked Questions (FAQ) for the
newsgroup soc.college.fiancnail-aid

Funding Your Education: The Student Guide
http://www.ed.gov/prog_info/SFA/StudentGuide/The Student Guide
An overview of the Student Financial Assistance Programs of the
U.S. Department of Education, designed for high school students
and others entering a postsecondary school for the first time

Free Application for Federal Student Aid (FAFSA) Express
http://www.ed.gov/offices/OPE/express.html
On-line Windows-based financial aid application program from the
Department of Education

Sources of Free Information About Student Aid and Scholarship Search Services
http://www.ed.gov/prog_info/SFA/LSA/#services
From the U.S. Department of Education

The Student Guide 1996-97
http://www.ed.gov/prog_info/SFA/StudentGuide/
U.S. Department of Education information about student financial
assistance for the 1996-97 award year

Looking for Student Aid
http://www.finaid.org/finaid/documents/ed.html
A concise introduction to sources of free information about student
aid and scholarship search services, from the U.S. Department of
Education

Financial Aid for Students with Disabilities
http://www.finaid.org/finaid/documents/heath.html
From Health Resource Center of the American Council on Education

College Money Matters
http://www.signet.com/collegemoney
From Signet Bank overview of the whole higher education money game

Resource Pathways College Information Community
http://www.collegeguides.com/
Recommendations for financial auid resources

Loans and Scholarships

FinAid
http://www.cs.cmu.edu/afs/cs/user/mkant/public/finaid/finaid.htmla
A comprehensive guide to student financial aid, by the National Association of Student Financial Aid Administrators (NASFAA)

FinAid Undergraduate Scholarship and Fellowship Databases
http://www.finaid.org/finaid/awards.html

Financial Aid Information from Nellie Mae
http://www.nelliemae.org
From the largest non-profit provider of educational loan funds

Educaid Online
http://www.educaid.com/
Government student loan programs available, from an issuer of government guaranteed loans

Financial Aid Search Through the Web (FASTWEB)
http://web.studentservices.com/fastweb/
"The Internet's largest free (US) scholarship search"

Schools and Money, "The Ultimate College Survival Guide"
http://www.taponline.com/tap/higher.html
Study guides and libraries on the WWW, with a database of more than 180,000 scholarships, grants fellowships, and loans for college students living in the U.S

Scholarship Scam Alert
http://www.finaid.org/finaid/scams.html
"If you must pay money to get money, it might be a scam"

Federal Information Exchange (FEDIX) Minority On-Line Information Service (MOLIS)
http://web.fie.com/web/mol/
Information about minority institutions, including a database of scholarship and fellowship opportunities for minority students

Taxes

Income Tax Information On the Internet
http://www.best.com/~ftmexpat/html/taxsites.html

OTHER RESOURCES

Colleges/Universities

Links to all colleges
http://collegesuccess.com/college7.htm

College and University Home Pages
http://www.mit.edu:8001/people/cdemello/univ.html

U.S. Colleges and Universities–Geographical
http://www.utexas.edu/world/univ/alpha/
Listings organized geographically by state, then alphabetically by institution.

U.S. Colleges and Universities–Alphabetical
http://www.utexas.edu/world/univ/state/
Same listing as above but organized alphabetically by institution.

Community College Web
http://www.mcli.dist.maricopa.edu/cc/
Listings organized alphabetically and geographically, with a search engine

U.S. Two-Year Colleges
http://www.sp.utoledo.edu/twoyrcol.html
"The Most Complete List Available," organized geographically by state.

Community Colleges by State
http://www.utexas.edu/world/comcol/state/
Geographical listing of community colleges, maintained by The University of Texas, Austin.

Minority Institution Information
http://web.fie.com/web/mol/sql/molis.htm
Geographical and alphabetical listings of minority colleges in the United States

Test Companies

Educational Testing Service
http://www.ets.org
Home of the SAT, GRE, GMAT, TOEFL, and LSAT tests. Includes practice test questions

College Board Online

http://cbweb1.collegeboard.org/index.html

Graduate Records Examinations Board home page

http://www.gre.org/

Testprep.com

http://www.testprep.com/

Home page of Stanford Testing Systems, Inc. offering an online practice version of the SAT and review lessons